Educating
the Baccalaureate
Social Worker

Educating the Baccalaureate Social Worker

Report of the Undergraduate Social Work Curriculum Development Project

Betty L. Baer
and
Ronald Federico

Ballinger Publishing Company • Cambridge, Massachusetts
A Subsidiary of J.B. Lippincott Company

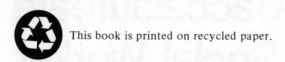

This book is printed on recycled paper.

This research was supported by a grant from the Department of Health, Education and Welfare, Social and Rehabilitation Service, Public Services Administration, under the authority of Public Law Section 426 of the Social Security Act.

The views expressed in this report are not necessarily those of the funding source or the School of Social Work at West Virginia University.

International Standard Book Number: 0-88410-666-7

Library of Congress Catalog Card Number: 77-16189

Printed in the United States of America

Library of Congress Cataloging in Publication Data

West Virginia. University Undergraduate Social Worker Curriculum Development
    Project. Educating the baccalaureate social worker.

    1. Social work education. 2. Social work education—Curricula. I. Baer, Betty.
II. Federico, Ronald. III. Title.
HV11.W48A55   375'.361   77-16189
ISBN 0-88410-666-7

Advisory Task Force Membership

UNDERGRADUATE SOCIAL WORK
CURRICULUM DEVELOPMENT PROJECT

E. CLIFFORD BRENNAN
Virginia Commonwealth University
School of Social Work
Richmond, Virginia

LAURA BROWN-JOLLIFFE
Family Service Association
Morgantown, West Virginia

KAY DEA
University of Utah
School of Social Work
Salt Lake City, Utah

MIRIAM DINERMAN
Rutgers University
School of Social Work
New Brunswick, New Jersey

JACQUELINE D. FASSETT
Sinai Hospital of Baltimore, Inc
Baltimore, Maryland

DONALD FELDSTEIN*
Fairleigh-Dickinson University
Center for Social Work and
   Applied Social Research
Teaneck, New Jersey

HILDA HIDALGO
Livingston College–Rutgers
Department of Community
   Development
New Brunswick, New Jersey

LESTER I. LEVIN
United Jewish Federation
Buffalo, New York

LAURA MORRIS
Family Service Association of
   Greater Boston
Boston, Massachusetts

WINIFRED O'HARA
Texas Department of Public Welfare
Austin, Texas

JAMES SATTERWHITE
Human Resources Administration
New York, New York

WILL SCOTT
Texas Southern University
Department of Sociology
Houston, Texas

*Now employed by the Federation of Jewish Philanthropies of New York City.

MARGARET SEBASTIAN
Ohio University
Department of Social Work
Athens, Ohio

BRAD SHEAFOR
Colorado State University
Department of Social Welfare
Fort Collins, Colorado

DON THOMAS
Louisiana Division of Family Services
New Orleans, Louisiana

EDWARD WEAVER
American Public Welfare Association
Washington, D.C.

CHARLES WRIGHT
Illinois Department of Mental Health
  and Developmental Disabilities
Decatur, Illinois

JOHN YANKEY
Case Western Reserve University
School of Applied Social Sciences
Cleveland, Ohio

RALPH DOLGOFF
CSWE Consultant
Council on Social Work Education
New York City.

Contents

Preface

The study reported on in this volume is of enormous potential significance for social work education and, thus, for professional practice. It is at once timely and organically linked to five previous major studies that have examined content, method, and structure in social work education.[1]

The timeliness of this undertaking can best be appreciated when viewed within the perspective of the rapidity with which baccalaureate education for social work has developed as a recognized level of professional education. Although baccalaureate education for social work is far from new, its graduates were accepted into full membership in the professional association as recently as 1970, and professional accreditation of baccalaureate programs of social work education was not inaugurated until 1974. Profound educational issues immediately came to the fore:

- What tasks, functions, and roles are carried by the baccalaureate social worker?
- What is the nature of the judgments and decisions such workers are called upon to make?
- With what degree of autonomy should they practice social work?
- What educational objectives concerning needed knowledge, values, and skills flow from answers to the preceding questions?
- What kinds of learning experiences can be offered to assist students in attaining these objectives?
- What resources are required to mount and sustain such a program?
- What faculty competencies are needed?

- What relationships with practice would be mutually supportive?
- What is the optimal administrative structure of a baccalaureate social work program within a college or university?
- What are the implications for other levels of social work education in delineation of the desired baccalaureate program?

If the world were as orderly as one might wish, all of these issues and many more would have been resolved prior to the implementation of a dual level system of entry into the profession. However, history does not wait for order, and the full answer to many of these issues will never be available. No single study can approach them all.

The potential value of this study is suggested by the active contributions from practice, as well as from education, which characterized its process. No previous curriculum study had elicited so thorough an amalgam of the contributions of both the practice and academic wings of the profession. Another salient characteristic of the study lies in the specificity and range of its recommendations. Such specificity invites engagement on the part of the reader; it will be the rare social worker or social work educator who will not feel impelled to add to, subtract from, or otherwise modify some of the recommendations. It is precisely the detail that is offered here which, if viewed as nonprescriptive, as its authors clearly intend, is suggestive of the stimulating aid the volume can be to newly developing educational programs, as well as to established programs that are engaged in review of their curriculum.

The CSWE standards for baccalaureate education[2] describe the curriculum areas which the Council on Social Work Education's Commission on Accreditation, Board of Directors, and House of Delegates see as essential components of a sound educational program for baccalaureate social work. The CSWE was pleased to provide consultative services to this project in recognition of its rich potential for interpreting and explicating these accreditation standards, as well as for testing their validity.

It has been frequently observed that the fate of many studies is to rest unexamined and unused. While it is important to note that the recommendations contained in this report are not official positions of the CSWE or of its Commission on Accreditation, the Commission on Educational Planning has already declared its intent to use this report, and other materials, as important aids in carrying out its charge to explicate the "base" content that all professional social workers should have, as well as in its deliberations of the report's implications for other levels of social work education. The Commission on Accreditation is preparing to review this report toward the end of determining which of its recommendations offer guidelines for better implementation of existing accreditation standards.

Any curriculum study is a somewhat risky venture; strong attachments exist to current arrangements. Part of the significance for professional education in the present report is in the continuity it provides with what has preceded it and in its authors' willingness to take positions, derived from the contributions of a broadly based and diverse group of participants.

Richard Lodge
Executive Director
Council on Social Work Education

1. Werner Boehm, "Education for Social Work: Studies," in *Encyclopedia of Social Work, Volume 1* (New York: National Association of Social Workers, 1977), p. 300.

2. *Standard for the Accreditation of Baccalaureate Degree Programs in Social Work* (New York: Council on Social Work Education, #74-210-19).

 *Chapter 1*

Foreword and Introduction

The Undergraduate Social Work Curriculum Development Project was funded to the School of Social Work at West Virginia University for the purpose of improving and strengthening curricula at the undergraduate level. More specifically, the goal became that of further explicating both educational objectives and the curriculum content essential to the achievement of those objectives. This report represents the results of our efforts to achieve these goals.

The goals represented an awesome charge for us. However, as we began our work and moved through the two years of activity that this report reflects, we recognized that we had the opportunity to learn from and build upon the work of colleagues in earlier curriculum development studies. Many of those studies, which are acknowledged elsewhere in this report, had goals similar to this project. All of them contributed to our work. Thus, we came to see our effort as part of an ongoing curriculum-building process in social work education directed toward further defining and refining the basics, or fundamentals, for entry level professional practice in social work. Hopefully this report, which represents the deliberations of many practitioners and educators, will make a substantial contribution to that continuing process.

There are some critical differences between the work of this project and others that have preceded it. First, it is the first curriculum project, national in scope, to take place since 1969, when the National Association of Social Workers admitted the graduates of CSWE-approved baccalaureate programs to full membership in

1

2 Educating the Baccalaureate Social Worker

the profession as entry level professional practitioners. Similarly, it is the first project to focus on the baccalaureate level of education since the Council on Social Work Education began accrediting baccalaureate programs in July 1974. These factors contributed to the urgency felt throughout social work education and the entire profession for greater definition and clarity regarding the basic content essential for entry level professional practitioners in social work.

Second, the project utilized a curriculum development strategy that aimed to develop the potential for a rich and productive relationship between practitioners and educators, who needed to serve as full partners in the project's curriculum development activity, since the ultimate objective for the professional educational program is to prepare persons for competent practice. We believe that the project demonstrates the importance and the viability of practitioners and educators working together as equals toward the achievement of the common objective. All of the project materials have been developed out of the contributions and criticisms of both groups. In the process, many of the myths each had about the other were dispelled, and a warm regard developed out of the recognition that a curriculum that does indeed aim to prepare for basic practice demands the contributions and support of practitioners and educators alike.

Third, the project aimed to secure some measure of consensus in what the entry level practitioner ought to be prepared to do. This, insofar as we are aware, has never been attempted before on a national level. We felt that there could not be a specific delineation of objectives or definition of curriculum content for the basic entry level practitioner unless there was some agreement within the profession and social work education on the practice expectations for this level worker. Hopefully, the project's work in this area will be helpful to the whole of social work education, as well as to the practice community. The manner in which the project went about accomplishing this particular task is described in the scope and methodology section of the report (Chapter 4).

Finally, in presenting the findings, we have attempted to state the positions taken by the project as openly and candidly as possible. We thought it essential that all those who might utilize the material understand the stance taken by the project, particularly in areas where the profession as a whole has not achieved consensus.

When positions are known and stated, there can be continued deliberation and debate.

ORGANIZATION OF THE REPORT

This report is divided into three main parts. The first part is made up of Chapters 2 and 3, each of which stands on its own, although material from Chapter 3 was utilized as a backdrop piece for Chapter 10 (Summary and Implications). These chapters deal with the following areas: Chapter 2, Significance of the Project for the Profession; and Chapter 3, The Current State of Baccalaureate Social Work Programs.

The remaining chapters constitute a whole, with each building on previous chapters. They make up the second part of the report, which is also the report's main body. Chapter 4, Project Objectives and Methodology, presents background information and discusses the methodology utilized by the project. This is critical for understanding how subsequent sections of the report were developed. Chapter 5, Practice Perspectives Related to Social Work Education, has a paper written by a practitioner member of the project task force which presents major issues of concern to practitioners that are also relevant to the educational preparation of future practitioners. This paper is followed by a summarization by project staff of the issues raised by the BSW practitioners who participated in the workshop held specifically to seek their contributions. Chapter 6 identifies the assumptions, or positions, taken by the project. It also includes a glossary of terms, as well as the project's definition of social work. Clearly, the assumptions served as a guide and as a screen for the subsequent curriculum development activity. Chapter 7, Objectives, Functions, and Activities for Entry Level Professional Practice in Social Work, aims to define what the entry level practitioner should be prepared to do. Material in this chapter was utilized to develop Chapter 8, The Competencies of the Entry Level Professional Social Worker. It needs to be emphasized here that the material in Chapter 7 was developed only to guide the identification and selection of the competencies needed by the entry level worker. It is included in the project report as an aid to understanding how and why the ten basic competencies were selected. Building from the competencies identified in Chapter 8, Chapter 9, Knowledge, Values, and Skills Essential for the Attainment of the Entry Level Competencies, summarizes each of the knowledge, values, and skills components of a baccalaureate curriculum. Finally, the main body of the report includes, in Chapter 10, a summary of the major project findings and a discussion of some of their implications for the future strengthening of educational programs for preparing entry level practitioners.

The third part of the report includes three appendixes. Appendix C is a listing of all persons who acted as consultants for the project. A complete elaboration of the knowledge, values, and skills essential for the attainment of the entry level competencies is given in Appendix B. Appendix A comprises four position papers on issues of significance to social work education. The importance of these papers is discussed in the introduction to the appendices.

ACKNOWLEDGMENTS

In a very real sense, the findings presented here represent the contributions of many persons.

If the work of this project results in a significant contribution to social work education, to practice, and to the delivery of more effective services to people, it will be because of the enthusiasm, the concern, the contributions, and the support of our colleagues in practice and in education around the country, given in the conviction that all of us have a responsibility and an obligation to contribute to the strengthening of social work education. Project staff carried final responsibility for the writing and organization of the report as it is presented here. We hope that we have presented the many helpful contributions from our friends and colleagues in a manner that does justice to all of them. If there are omissions, the fault is ours, not theirs.

Along with all of the individuals who are identified by name elsewhere in this report, we want to specifically acknowledge the dedication and hard work of the members of the project's advisory task force. The group held three formal meetings during the two year period (July 1975–July 1977). In between meetings, individual members of the task force were frequently called upon to assist with project-sponsored workshops and meetings, to act as consultants in discussing issues and problems, and to react to drafts of materials. They also suffered with us through our "ups and downs," and more than any group, made the final outcome as it is presented here possible.

We owe special thanks to Dr. Richard Lodge, executive director of the Council on Social Work Education, and to members of his staff. They understood the difficulties of the task and consistently provided encouragement and support. During the first year of the project, Dr. Miriam Dinerman served as special consultant to the project from the Council on Social Work Education. Dr. Ralph Dolgoff served in this capacity during the second year. Both of these individuals served the project well and merit special recognition.

Jacqueline D. Fassett and Charles Wright served as liaison between the National Association of Social Workers and the project. We were fortunate indeed that these two individuals were designated to represent NASW. They became not only active and articulate members of the project's task force, but also invaluable in their counsel to us in matters related to the project's relationship with the profession. Chauncy Alexander, executive director of NASW, and other members of the NASW staff conferred with project staff on many occasions and participated in several of the task force and workshop sessions. They reflected the concern of the profession that the educational preparation of the entry level practitioner be strengthened within the context of the mission and ethics of the profession.

One of the earliest contacts made by the project director was with Edward T. Weaver, executive director of the American Public Welfare Association. This turned out to be a fruitful contact and one that greatly enriched the project's work. Mr. Weaver generously made himself and the resources of the American Public Welfare Association available to the project whenever called upon.

We want also to acknowledge the contribution of our many colleagues in baccalaureate education across the country. Wherever we went, there were inquiries and expressions of support. They have participated in the struggle toward the achievement of full recognition for the baccalaureate social worker; they served to remind us of the importance of our work to help them in their efforts to strengthen the programs with which they are identified.

This project would never have existed had it not been for Dr. Pauline Godwin, special assistant to the commissioner and director of the Office of State Management and Training, Administration for Public Services, of the Department of Health, Education and Welfare. She, and the late Seth Lowe, who served as the federal liaison with the project from its inception until his illness forced his retirement in September 1976, were consistent in their support of us and in their convictions regarding the value of the baccalaureate social worker in the nation's service delivery system.

The project director wishes to acknowledge with appreciation the support given to her by Dr. Barbara K. Shore, director of the

doctoral program of the University of Pittsburgh, and Anne Minahan and Allen Pincus at the University of Wisconsin, Madison. Anne
Minahan read the final document in its entirety and made many
helpful suggestions.

Finally, but not least, we acknowledge with appreciation the
support of our colleagues in the School of Social Work of West
Virginia University and in the Social Work Program of the University
of North Carolina at Greensboro. We were relieved of our other
responsibilities in order to carry out the project's work. Professors
Jeanne M. Hunzeker and Robert Jones served as recorders for several
of the workshops. Debbie Imling, Jerry Dobbs, Rita Rendina, Viola
Smith, and Sherry Thomas provided faithful clerical support.

BETTY L. BAER
Project Director
and
RONALD FEDERICO
Project Associate

September 15, 1977

 *Chapter 2*

Significance of the Project for the Profession

Chauncey A. Alexander

The definition of the basic curriculum for the baccalaureate social work (BSW) degree will be another landmark in the history of the development of the social work profession and in the establishment of competence requirements for the delivery of social services. It will settle some practice and education dilemmas, but it will also open the door to many more professional problems.

The BSW curriculum project recommendations should provide the baseline of practice competence that will denote entry into the profession. At the same time, the project will stimulate work on the differentiation of various levels of professional and nonprofessional tasks. It should have a great impact on master's programs in the graduate schools of social work, particularly in facilitating consideration of the specialization questions in education and practice. If present conditions and needs continue, it will stimulate the completion of the task of rationalizing the labor force and service delivery in the social services.

Nothing in the social work profession has created the controversy, aroused emotions, and been subjected to as much debate as the growth of the BSW degree and practitioner, with the possible exception of the practice-policy dichotomy. The BSW development has been characterized as a "watering-down of the profession"; a lowering of the acceptance and recognition of social work; a deprofessionalization of social work practice; and an economic move to increase NASW income and bolster the enrollment of the schools of social work. Advocates of the development of the BSW curriculum and degree counter that it instead has raised the value and status of the MSW, pointing to the differentiation in legal regulation and the economic advantages of the ACSW certification. They point out that the declassification moves in some states have been opportunistic political attacks on professional training per se as a criterion for job classification, rather than being limited to a choice between MSW and BSW.

Instead of "deprofessionalization," it is argued that the differential classification of tasks and responsibilities has increased professional accountability. The increased quality assurance achieved through the ACSW examination, the NASW Clinical Social Workers Register, and the standards set in such governmental programs as CHAMPUS, PSRO's, HMO's and others are cited. It is also a fact that NASW has reaped additional costs and accountability requirements much greater than the income and that the schools of social work have no lack of applicants.

Although all of these controversies represent important elements in a profession's growth process, they tend to ignore the fact that this development was and is, to a great extent, inevitable. It is a reflection of more powerful social and economic forces than the individual desire or will of members of a profession. It is the result of the need for the rationalization (the application of modern methods of efficiency) of an increasingly complex and gigantic social services industry. The emergence of the social work profession as a concomitant of the complex industrialized society, with its values rooted in democratic and humanitarian philosophies, has been well documented. It is also generally accepted that the contradictions and dysfunctions of the present postindustrial capitalist society require organizational forms and a professional and technical labor force to help people deal with the problems that affect the quality of life.

Today, social work as a professional discipline has penetrated nearly every aspect of people's lives in the United States. Social workers are found not just in child and family agencies or medical settings but in all societal institutions—in government, health, industrial, educational, recreational, and judicial systems—where some collision between the individual and the institutions have required special attention to meet people's problems. The fact that professional social work is not the only accepted helping profession in these various institutional arrangements can be explained by the variable history of each societal institution and its response to people's needs and by the self-imposed limitations of the social work profession.

Nevertheless, social work meets all the criteria as a learned profession and is finding increasing acceptance and status in society. The profession has acquired an extensive body of transmissible theoretical and practical knowledge; it receives the community sanction demonstrated in state licensing and an extensive public and voluntary agency system; it is recognized by a growing clientele; it requires adherence to a code of ethics and other professional standards for self-discipline; and it has a professional culture sustained by formal association (NASW). The differentiation of levels and types of functions internal to the profession is a further clarification and consolidation of professional practice.

THE PRESENT STATUS OF THE BSW PRACTITIONER

The social services industry consists of more than 48,000 governmental and voluntary agencies providing an infinite variety of national, state, and local services.[1] An undetermined, though growing, number of private, for profit organizations that have entered the field in recent years and either directly or indirectly provide social services must be added to the nonprofit group. The private, for profit sector of the industry has been broadened by some 12,000 social workers in private practice, of which approximately 1,500 to 2,000 are in full-time practice.[2] Practitioners with BSW degrees permeate all of these social services but are found particularly in the public welfare agencies and, more recently, in health settings.

The labor force for the social services industry is estimated at this time to be a minimum of 352,000 workers.[3] Of that number, 110,000, or 31 percent, are estimated to have graduate social work degrees.[4] Approximately 40 percent, or 140,000, are estimated to have bachelor's degrees, of which approximately 55,000 are graduates of social welfare curricula.[5] Of the 102,000 left, it is estimated that 43,000 have some college education.[6] If these ratios are near correct, then 15.6 percent of the present labor force are BSWs.

The significance of the BSW entry into this labor force and the potential for the eventual alteration of the ratios of MSWs, BSWs, and nonprofessional personnel may be seen in the fact that as of November 1, 1976, there were 25,281 full-time degree students in 170 programs (16,255 in their junior or senior years in 169 programs) with 7,102 awarded BSW degrees. This was an increase of 398 over the previous year. As a comparative figure, 16,869 full-time students were enrolled in masters programs and 769 in postmasters, with 9,080 awarded masters degrees and 179 doctoral degrees.[7]

The BSW degree holder is accepted as a regular member of the NASW and has been since 1970 as the result of a vote via a national membership referendum. A special BSW committee is one of the national units and BSW's are represented as members on most of the others. The BSW is recognized as the professional entry degree in NASW's "Standards for Social Service Manpower," a six level personnel classification system for the field, as well as in the NASW model statute for licensing. Nine of the twenty states that have legal regulation of social workers specifically designate the BSW as a requirement in the law. Seven of those nine states have obtained legal regulation since 1972, when NASW began its nationwide drive. In addition, the NASW Competence Certification Board plans the development of a national BSW examination for use by the states in licensing at the BSW level.

Thus, as the foregoing demonstrates, the BSW degree and practitioners are an integral part of the collective of professional practioners.

THE BSW PRACTITIONERS—
A BRIEF REVIEW

Contrary to the impression of those who have suddenly discovered the BSW presence, such practitioners did not spring full grown from the head of Zeus. Their development into an accepted professional practitioner classification was the result of arduous debates and struggles in the education and practice sectors of the profession over at least twenty-five years. The history of this development in the educational sector has its own dynamics, beginning principally with the land grant colleges, and must be told elsewhere, even though obviously it is interrelated with practice.

The principal energizer for that development has been the persistent gap between the supply and demand for social services personnel, a gap that has been fueled by the escalating recognition of the need for social services and rising expectations of American citizens. It is important to remember that although this gap had always existed, it became critical at the initiation of social programs during the Great Depression. This personnel gap resulted in the strategy of meeting personnel demands by increasing the production of MSWs and by expanding in-service training in agencies, a strategy that still persists in many forms.

In the late 1940s and the 1950s, the general direction was to utilize volunteers or to provide in-service training to nonprofessionals under the supervision of masters degree workers. During this period, agencies began to experiment with the use of "indigenous" personnel to supplement or substitute for MSWs. Many different attempts were made in various agencies to differentiate the work levels and requirements with many exaggerated claims and heated debates over the efficacy of this approach.

It was during this period that the 1956 Amendments to the Social Security Act (Title VII, sec. 705) first authorized the use of federal funds for the training of personnel in public assistance. Although the same strategy of training MSWs was followed, this development laid the economic base for the eventual support of baccalaureate training. That no article on this matter appears in the *Social Work* journal from 1956 to 1961 is a significant indicator of the lag created by the exclusive MSW policy of the professional association at that time.

This situation changed rapidly during the 1960 decade, and the trends in personnel utilization of the early 1960s are reported in detail by Barker and Briggs.[8] However, for immediate purposes, it is worthwhile to note the early confusion and the eventual emergence of two streams of other than the MSW-trained personnel in social services, one originating as the "subprofessional" (performs functions *auxiliary* to the professional), and the other the "nonprofessional" or "indigenous" (performs functions *separate* from the professional). The rapid expansion of social services beginning with the administration of President Kennedy was an important factor in generating practice and education developments with both classes of personnel.

The moves toward differential classification appear to have begun with agency experimentation, first reported by Monahan,[9] Heyman,[10] Weed and Denham,[11] and Calnan[12]. The Heyman study of the utilization of personnel at Albert Einstein Medical Center in Philadelphia, the Veterans Administration study of the use of social work assistants, and the Schwartz research to develop and test ways of improving the organization and use of public assistance personnel (later published in 1972 by the NASW[13]) are illustrative of the early larger efforts at differentiating social work responsibilities that led to the professionalization of the BSW. Demonstration research projects and individual agency experiments continued to proliferate, particularly in the local public welfare agencies and in large private agencies, as did the literature.

The social work profession responded organizationally to these developments with the establishment in 1961 of an NASW Subcommittee on Utilization of Personnel of the National Commission on Practice. This subcommittee developed the dimensions of client vulnerability and worker autonomy as differentiating criteria for different levels of personnel utilization.[14] A basic contribution to the development of interest and the focusing of manpower issues was the NASW publication "Manpower in Social Welfare: Research Perspectives," which resulted from an Institute on Research Approaches to Manpower Problems in Social Welfare Services to Children and Families held at the University of Minnesota, Duluth, August 1964.[15] This publication covered trends and projections, the welfare system, the professional system, and career choice and education. However, it emphasized the shortages and focused on the master's programs. It tended to ignore the differential classification question and the potential of baccalaureate education as a resource.

However, an important leverage toward recognition of a BSW classification came from the Barker and Briggs study previously cited. This study of mental health social workers in the Connecticut Valley State Hospital and twenty selected hospital units resulted in the demonstration of the improvement of the quality and quantity of practice with the use of non-MSWs, easing the shortage of professional social workers and expanding the range of service that could be provided effectively. It made clear the options of the non-MSW as an ancillary worker and of the BSW graduate as a beginning professional.

A most significant event of this period was the publication by the U.S. Department of Health, Education and Welfare of the report of its Departmental Task Force on Social Work Education and Manpower entitled "Closing the Gap in Social Work Manpower."[16] This comprehensive report projected escalating demands for social workers and clearly delineated two classifications in social work: masters and baccalaureate degree workers. It called for (1) the tripling of the annual number of graduates with the development of new schools; (2) the continuation of two classifications of social work manpower—MSW and baccalaureate; (3) scholarship aid and loans to facilitate recruitment; (4) professional recognition of both classifications of social worker by the professional membership organization through broadened membership eligibility and by state government licensing; (5) definition and delineation of functions of ancillary and technical personnel; (6) improvement of salaries and career opportunities; and (7) the development of accurate, comprehensive information on current supply, distribution, and utilization of personnel. This document played an exceptional role in focusing attention on the social work labor force problems and in advocating the BSW degree as a recognized professional classification.

The recognition by the profession of the BSW practitioner is revealed in their brief summary of the NASW Delegate Assembly actions:

1964—A proposal "to involve all social workers in the program of the NASW" was referred for study and report at the next assembly. An unofficial voting by the delegates to include other "workers in social welfare" in the framework of NASW resulted in 178 'no' votes, 111 'yes', and 66 abstentions. A large majority voted for no distinction by classes of membership should NASW be opened to "persons with AB degrees."

1967—The Commission on Certification and Membership reported that the results of their study "indicated an overwhelming majority of the chapters did not favor any change in membership requirements." A resolution was subsequently approved that established a committee to study the subject of broadened membership eligibility and to make specific recommendations prior to the next delegate assembly.

1969—Action was taken on membership eligibility to provide regular membership to "Any person who holds the baccalaureate degree, having completed an undergraduate program in social work that meets the criteria established by the Council on Social Work Education."

A national membership referendum in 1969 resulted in approval and implementation in 1970, with subsequent action by the Council of Social Work Education on the establishment of criteria for undergraduate programs, followed by the development of accreditation criteria and programs.

Implementation of this decision and vote through recruitment and participation of BSWs in NASW did not come easily. There were pockets of resistance in chapter leadership and sizeable sections of the MSW membership who cited some of their experiences with BSW graduates and the quality of some schools as verification of the nonprofessional nature of BSW practice. This resistance seemed to center in areas where practitioners had not been close to the shift of social work education to the undergraduate level, and with some graduate schools.

The NASW moved rapidly to implement the conception of rationalization of the social services labor force with the development of a six level differential classification system for the field, including four professional levels: Social Worker (BSW), Graduate Social Worker (MSW), Certified Social Worker (ACSW), and Social Work Fellow (doctorate or ACSW plus two years specialized experience).

Two preprofessional levels were delineated: Social Service Aide (maturity and life experience) and Social Service Technician (AA degree in social services or other baccalaureate degree).[17] The BSW has thus been firmly established, and despite the need to formulate operational definitions in some settings to clearly differentiate BSW practitioner functions from those of MSWs, it constitutes the professional entry degree. This clarification of the place of the BSW was also reinforced by its incorporation in the NASW model statute for licensing with the results previously reported. It was made one of the requirements for support of any state licensing legislation by the action of the national Board of Directors on October 23, 1976.[18]

THE FUTURE OF THE BSW PRACTITIONER

If, as Burke has said, you can never plan the future by the past, we must despair for the opportunity to avoid the confusions and mistakes regarding the differential classification of social work practice. On the other hand, if we subscribe to the view of Patrick Henry that "I know no way of judging the future but by the past," we can proceed with confidence. As some of our most profound decision-makers say: It all depends. If there is strong governmental response to the many social problems, the need for professional and technical social service personnel will escalate, with a resultant heavy demand for BSWs and MSWs. If the Council on Social Work Education and the schools of social work utilize the curriculum project recommendations to produce better professionals for the field, and if the social services advocates (citizens, clients, and the organized profession) demand better quality and more effective service, then the role and use of the BSW will be rapidly consolidated.

It should be apparent that clarity regarding the functions and tasks of the BSW graduate will provide the baseline, the measure, for many other practice developments. The most immediate use for the practice sector will be to strengthen the fight against "declassification," an opportunistic and retrogressive program initiated by the Nixon administration. The NASW 1977 Delegate Assembly supported its national office efforts in this regard by placing it as highest on its list of program priorities.

The NASW program thrust to improve professional standards in social services delivery is being escalated to establish a basic level of competence in the social services through state licensing, guaranteed by nationally standardized examinations at the BSW level. Paralleling this activity is the development of competence examinations for specialty areas of social work practice, beginning with the clinical social work area, an activity which in itself depends upon determining what is fundamental in practice. Another supportive effort has been the increased attention to the requirement for ethical practice and the invocation of the NASW Code of Ethics through the complaint adjudication procedures. The concentration on production of practice standards, such as standards for social service departments in hospitals for School Social Workers, and for PSROs, HMOs, and others, is helping to define and consolidate the differential classification system.

Again, there is no question but that the benchmark BSW will contribute to the theory and knowledge development in social work. Even if the definition is not perfect, it provides a testing and departure point against which research can begin. Given this baseline of generic practice, the clarification of specialization and specialty interests in social work practice initiated by NASW, and now the charge to a special NASW-CSWE Task Force, will assume even greater importance and timeliness. The provision of a base or takeoff point for continuing education conducted by NASW national and chapter units, schools of social work, and social agencies that is thus created will be another far-reaching outcome.

For the NASW and the CSWE, a BSW curriculum standard strengthens their programs for a revitalized national policy of federal leadership in the development of the professional and technical labor force of the nation. Such a program translates into the creation of data systems on the social services labor force, national services and personnel planning, financial support of students and schools, and other such measures. For the NASW, it provides a clarification that improves its ability to carry forward its action program to improve national, state, and local social policies and programs. It further helps clarify the standards to be introduced into legislation and the best forms of service delivery to be recommended.

The proposed BSW curriculum still has to win the approval of the profession, of NASW on one side and CSWE on the other. Since this project has used most of the devices of participation, its eventual passage should be assured. For the NASW, the proposal will be exposed for review and debate via its publications and its national and chapter units to as many practitioners as possible. The reactions from the field will be gathered and consolidated into a position paper that may involve some recommended alterations. These will be subject to action by the national board of directors. Assuming a position representing the practice sector is reached, it will then go to the NASW-CSWE Joint Board Committee for mutual consideration. It will then presumably tie into the CSWE process, with NASW input at appropriate points.

With this overall perspective goes the conviction that the social work profession has the opportunity to make a qualitative leap in its practice development and its maturity as a learned profession. That conviction also carries the hope that all practitioners will understand and support the practice differentiations necessary to build a truly unified profession.

NOTES

1. Based on estimates of the American Association of Fundraising Counsel and the United Way.

2. Based on professional liability insurance coverage under NASW's program.

3. U.S. Bureau of Census, *1970 Subject Reports:* Final report PC(2)-7A, *Occupational Characteristics,* Table 5 (Washington, D.C.: Government Printing Office) Reports 222, 493 plus an average of 15,000 per annum additional positions to 1977 plus 25,000 administrators, supervisors, and undercounts not included in census figures.

4. *Salaries and Working Conditions of Social Welfare in 1960* (New York: National Social Welfare Assembly, 1960), Table 18, estimates 19,686 plus 11,000 undercounts plus 82,779 MSW graduates since 1960 minus 3 percent dropouts (3,404).

5. *1970 Subject Reports.* Using 68 percent (as shown in the 1970 census) having bachelor's degrees or above times the 352,000 total less the 110,000 MSWs and BSW graduate figures.

6. Ibid. Using 1970 data showing 41.7 percent having college work.

7. *Statistics on Social Work Education in the United States: 1976* (New York: Council on Social Work Education, 1977), p. 18, 22.

8. Barker, Robert L., and Thomas L. Briggs, *Differential Use of Social Work Manpower* (New York: National Association of Social Workers, 1968), p. 32-51.

9. Monahan, Fergus T., A Study of Non-Professional Personnel in Social Work—The Army Social Work Specialist (Washington, D.C.: Catholic University of America Press, 1960).

10. Heyman, Margaret M., "A Study of Effective Utilization of Social Workers in a Hospital Setting," *Social Work* 6, 2 (April 1961): 36-43.

11. Weed, Verne, and William H. Denham, "Toward More Effective Use of the Non-Professional Worker: A Recent Experiment," *Social Work* 6, 4 (October 1961): 29-36.

12. Calnan, Wilfred M., "The Use of Social Work Aides in a State Mental Hospital," NIMH Project OM 137, February, 1961 (mimeographed).

13. Schwartz, Edward E., and William C. Sample, *The Midway Office* (New York: NASW, 1972).

14. "Utilization of Personnel in Social Work: Those With Full Professional

Education and Those Without" (New York: NASW, February 1962) (mimeographed).

15. Manpower in Social Welfare, Edward E. Schwartz, ed. (New York: NASW, 1966).

16. "Closing the Gap in Social Work Manpower" (Washington, D.C.: U.S. Department of Health, Education and Welfare, November 1965).

17. Standards for Social Service Manpower, NASW policy statement 4 (Washington, D.C.: NASW, June 1973).

18. Standards for the Regulation of Social Work Practice, NASW policy statement 5 (Washington, D.C.: NASW, October 1976).

Chapter 3

The Current State of Baccalaureate Social Work Programs

INTRODUCTION

The Curriculum Development Project undertook a review of the state of baccalaureate social work programs in the United States. This review was carried out in order to secure basic information about curriculum offerings and content of these programs.* Such information allows for a comparison of currently existing curriculum objectives and content with the project's findings with respect to the basic curriculum content needed to educate baccalaureate level professional social workers. From this comparison, and along with other project findings, implications for future curriculum development emerge. They are discussed in Chapter 10.

METHODOLOGY

This review of baccalaureate social work programs is based upon the examination of accreditation application documents, communications from the CSWE Commission on Accreditation to programs seeking accreditation, and other relevant documents. The identity of individual programs was appropriately disguised. The review, which includes programs granted accreditation as well as those that

---

*This review does not attempt to provide basic statistical information about numbers of programs, faculty, or students. This information is already available in *An Analysis of Undergraduate Social Work Programs Approved by CSWE, 1971*, prepared by Alfred Stamm in 1972 and scheduled for updating and publication in early 1978.

unsuccessfully sought accreditation, covered the period from the onset of accreditation (July 1, 1974) until January 1, 1977. In carrying out the review, Dr. Ralph Dolgoff, CSWE consultant to the project, reviewed the documents of some 300 different programs with which the commission had contact during this period of time. Of the 200 plus programs seeking accreditation during the first year of this process, 20 percent received the maximum five year accreditation; 35 percent were denied accreditation. Dr. Dolgoff was assisted in his work by the staff of the CSWE Division of Standards and Accreditation. Supplementary information was obtained through consultation with Alfred Stamm, director of the division.

It must be noted that the review findings represent summarization of self-reported and site visit information about programs, as well as a summarization of the findings of the Commission on Accreditation as it reviewed curricula against the accreditation standards. It needs to be emphasized that the major purpose of the accreditation process is to assure that a program is in minimal compliance with standards as mandated and interpreted at a particular time.

The Commission on Accreditation can only review programs according to the criteria mandated by the standards. The standards themselves are determined by the CSWE board of directors and the house of delegates. While the standards have not changed since the inception of accreditation in 1974, interpretations of the standards naturally do change from time to time. For example, at the onset of accreditation of baccalaureate programs, little attention was paid to the role and position of women in social work education. With the development of the guidelines for accreditation related to women in social work education, a result of board action, and the subsequent utilization of the guidelines by the Commission on Accreditation in reviewing programs, glaring deficiencies began to be noted. Yet, prior to that time, programs initially reviewed and accredited may have had similar deficiencies that passed unnoted. This is not a weakness of the accreditation process, but rather a strength. As the profession responds to new concerns and demands, so too does a viable accreditation process. It is pointed out here, however, as a factor that must be considered in reading the project's review of the accreditation documents. This is especially important since the period of time covered includes the historic beginning of the accreditation of baccalaureate programs, followed by subsequent years of strengthening and tightening the entire process.

Quite naturally, our review served to highlight areas of concern. The overall purpose of the curriculum project is to strengthen baccalaureate level curricula and that demands understanding and the recognition of shortcomings. The enormous strengths of baccalaureate education, not fully presented here, must also be recognized and appreciated. We have tried to emphasize that great strides have been made in a very short period of time. Perhaps the underlying and most significant strength of baccalaureate education is the willingness to recognize weaknesses and to seek ways to improve itself. Such a quality, obviously, does not appear in accreditation documents.

The review of programs as presented here represents the summarization of some of the strengths and shortcomings of baccalaureate social work programs as they have been identified by the Commission on Accreditation. The information presented is that perceived by those closely related to the project as most germane to the project and its work. Information is organized around the strengths and weaknesses found in programs seeking accreditation. Programs that were denied or granted only short-term accreditation reflect a greater number of these deficiencies and/or weaknesses, while programs granted longer terms of accreditation reflect more complete compliance with the standards, and, as a rule, are more fully developed.

CURRICULUM ISSUES

In presenting and discussing the major curriculum issues identified from a review of the documents described earlier, both particular strengths and commonly identified deficiencies will be noted. These issues represent a composite of those found in all the documents examined. Individual programs might include one or several of these issues, but no one program had all of these weaknesses or deficiencies.

Curriculum Integrity

One of the important issues identified was the degree to which a social work program in a college or university had control over its curriculum content. Control might become problematic in two ways. One is where the social work faculty does not have the primary responsibility for planning the curriculum content and direction. This sometimes occurs in host settings, where social work is part of another academic department (such as sociology); it can also occur in undergraduate programs located in graduate schools of social work. In the former instance, this issue may decrease in significance in the future given the trend toward social work programs becoming independent departments.

A program's control over its own content can be reduced in a second way when required foundation content is taught in other departments. The social work program may be able to require courses in other departments, but may have little influence on the actual content of what is taught, with the result that students do not have the needed foundation by the time they enter social work courses. More and more programs are attempting to insure that required foundation content taught in lower division courses is adequate to prepare students to progress in the social work program but effective influence on such content remains an issue.

A third problematic aspect of curriculum control for some programs is curriculum conceptualization. The interrelationship of curriculum content areas may be unclear, making it difficult to fit courses together into a cumulative sequence.

Faculty Resources

A number of issues concerning curriculum content are related to faculty resources. Assuming that each faculty member has limited areas of expertise, faculty in small departments may be forced to teach an unrealistic range of subjects, including some for which they are unprepared. This problem is exacerbated in programs where there are inadequate faculty resources for other program needs. In addition, faculty members may be kept too busy to teach any area well.

A related issue arises in programs where faculty members are inexperienced as educators. This issue may also arise with field instructors who lack sanctioned professional educational credentials such as a BSW or an MSW. However, this may reflect a healthy movement of baccalaureate programs into areas that have traditionally had limited numbers of social workers with sanctioned professional education. In such instances, standards require additional faculty time in assuring appropriate learning experiences.

Finally, there is sometimes an issue regarding the deployment of faculty resources. Even where there is an adequate number of faculty members, some may be used to teach specialized courses (often required when a program is funded by a grant) or to teach in other academic disciplines, leaving only a small number of other faculty to meet the demands of the basic curriculum.

Curriculum Objectives

Preparation for entry level practice is the major curriculum objective mandated for baccalaureate programs by accreditation standards. More and more programs are finding ways to identify specific practice outcomes around which curriculum content is then organized. However, there seems to be considerable difficulty in defining what practice at the entry level is. Many programs use a "generalist" perspective, but there is considerable variation and ambiguity about what this term means. Similar difficulties arise in the use of a "generic" perspective. Consequently, while expected practice outcomes are becoming more specific in many programs, there is limited uniformity of outcomes between programs.

Some programs reflect a lack of clarity regarding curriculum objectives and professional identity. The most common confusion in this area is between social work and human services. Accreditation standards require a clear social work identity, but a number of programs try to combine social work and human service objectives and content.

Related to this is the integration of professional socialization into curriculum objectives. In general, more and more programs are recognizing the need for strong professional socialization, since many baccalaureate social workers are employed in contexts where professional supervision is weak or absent. In such situations, strong self-direction and self-evaluation is important. The increasing number of hours in field instruction and the greater recognition of the need for a repertoire of meaningful practice skills are two ways in which this increasing emphasis on professional socialization is evidenced. However, professional socialization as a curriculum objective is often made more difficult for students that are members of diverse groups since few programs have instructors who are from these groups and who can provide strong role models.

A third issue regarding curriculum objectives is the frequently seen tension between basic program content and curriculum content for the development of specialized practice skills. Student and faculty interests, the requirements of grants, and the needs of a program's service area may all suggest the appropriateness of such specialized preparation. Accreditation standards allow for such content, but only as a logical and related extension of the base content. Problems arise when specialized preparation as a program objective leads to curriculum content contradictory to the basic conent or drains the program of resources needed to adequately teach the basic content.

Curriculum Content

A significant issue regarding curriculum content is the degree to which content is appropriate for curriculum objectives. A common problem occurs when content is too heavily weighted toward work with individuals and families, to the relative neglect of content on the larger, organizational context of human functioning and practice activities. Content about societal decisionmaking also tends to be weak. As a result, many programs view the difficulties people have in achieving their life goals as a consequence of individual pathology rather than seeing goal attainment as heavily influenced by group, organizational, community, and societal structures and processes. Such an unbalanced presentation of content makes it practically impossible to achieve a program objective of preparation for skill in a range of interventive modes as mandated by CSWE accreditation standards.

An overemphasis on individual and family content is particularly evident in four areas. Human behavior and the social environment content is most often structured around the life cycle, with emphasis on the years up to adulthood and relative neglect of adulthood and aging. Practice content is similarly unbalanced, with more time and emphasis given to clinical skills and intervention strategies than to skills and strategies appropriate to organizations, communities, and groups. This mitigates against the development of skills in a range of interventions, a necessary part of achieving a "generalist" objective. Content on social policy is also affected. The emphasis tends to be more descriptive than analytical, and there is limited use of political and economic knowledge that is immediately applicable to effective practice.

Finally, field placements tend to be consistent with the clinical methods focus, the majority of them primarily offering practice opportunities in casework settings. On the other hand, more and more programs have several types of experiential learning, so that not all such content is relegated to the field instruction course or courses. For example, many programs require observational and volunteer learning experiences before field instruction, thus increasing the student's opportunities to be exposed to practice in other than one-to-one and small group settings. However, there remains a continuing difficulty in many programs regarding the integration of field and class-based content. When this occurs, the utility of diverse field learning opportunities for helping students to develop a range of intervention skills is greatly diminished. In some programs, there may actually be a contradiction between what is taught in the field and what is taught in the classroom, to the detriment of both.

In spite of the continuing problem that many programs have in achieving a balance between individually oriented content and content related to organizations, groups, and communities, some progress is evident. Over the three years during which accreditation has been in operation, there has been a noticeable change toward the inclusion of more organization, group, and community content. This is true for both classroom and field-based learning.

A second curriculum content area that is generally troublesome is human diversity (content on ethnicity, race, women, lifestyle groups, and the handicapped). While all programs have some content in this area, it is usually primarily taught in one course. There is little integration of this content throughout the curriculum and little attention to the way in which the educational milieu reinforces or contradicts what content does exist. Most programs rely on courses taught in other departments, such as sociology or women's studies, to establish foundation content. However, the human diversity content fundamental to the program's curriculum objectives is usually only vaguely conceptualized, with a resultant lack of identity at all levels, and great variation in coverage and integration. The lack of a clear conceptualization of the meaning and significance of human diversity makes it difficult to achieve the objective of educating practitioners who are aware and respectful of such diversity. It also tends to promote the seemingly random overattention to certain diverse groups and the neglect of others.

As noted earlier, human behavior and social environment content is frequently problematic. The point has already been made that a sociocultural focus becomes difficult because of an overemphasis on individual and family dynamics. It has also been shown that the life cycle tends to be truncated, with the adult and aging phases generally neglected. An additional problem arises from the frequency with which the integration of human behavior and social environment content with the remainder of the curriculum fails to occur. Much of this content is frequently taught in other departments, such as sociology, psychology, political science, economics, and biology. To be effective in achieving program objectives related to practice preparation, such wide-ranging content needs to be integrated into the curriculum at appropriate points (such as its impact on methods, policy, and practice). Rather, such curriculum frequently is limited to somewhat variable, often elective courses teaching imprecisely defined content in so unsystematic a fashion that the student never learns to integrate it adequately.

As already suggested, supporting course content can be a difficulty for some programs. Lack of adequate influence on content taught in supporitng liberal arts courses often leads to uncertain learning in foundation areas for students. Consequently, many supporting course requirements become a ritual of fulfilling credits rather than providing precisely identified foundation content in areas such as the social sciences, biology, and communication skills. It is little wonder that many programs find it difficult to develop strategies for effectively integrating supporting content into the courses taught in the program itself. These problems are worsened in those programs that allow students a choice of courses to fulfill a given supporting area requirement. Unless the alternative courses are equivalent in their ability to teach specific content, which is highly unlikely, the problems of diverse and vaguely specified curriculum content become even more troublesome.

A final area of concern in curriculum content is research. The current norm is one research course, although more and more programs are requiring a statistics course as well. Most often, the research course is taught outside of the program, and the previously discussed problems of specification and integration of content arise once again. Inadequate demonstration of the applicability of this content to social work practice issues and concerns is especially evident as a problem. The use of research data from social work is not common, and the particular research needs of social work practitioners are not usually addressed. Consequently, research content can easily become too abstract and seemingly irrelevant for social work students.

Articulation

Although a continuum model for social work education is often conceptualized, it does not often seem to be operationalized. Indeed, most attention is paid to the baccalaureate-graduate part of the continuum, where accreditation standards require linkages when appropriate to a baccalaureate program's location and structural arrangements. This end of the continuum also seems to be a natural area of concern for baccalaureate program faculty and students, since the graduate level is perceived as having concrete rewards in terms of prestige and employment opportunities.

However, it may be the other end of the continuum that needs the most attention, and this seems to happen infrequently. Associate level programs have been developing rapidly and with little consistency as to focus and content. It is the graduates of these programs who are then moving into baccalaureate programs, and who are creating difficulties in terms of credit transfers and course equivalencies. While some baccalaureate programs have worked out reasonably stable relationships with associate-level programs, most have not. Until such relationships are developed, curriculum coherence and content integration for students moving between programs will be extremely difficult.

CONCLUSION

Obviously, baccalaureate social work programs across the country continue to struggle with a number of difficult curriculum content and resource issues. This is an unavoidable result of the very rapid growth and relatively recent initiation of the accreditation process and of the progressive learning, refinement, and reinterpretations that accompany such a process. From the project's perspective, those changes and issues that continue to be troublesome to programs are illuminating and helpful in identifying practice and curriculum issues of significance.

✳ *Chapter 4*

Project Objectives and Methodology

SCOPE AND METHODS OF THE PROJECT

The Charge to the Project

The broad objective of the Social and Rehabilitation Service of the Department of Health, Education, and Welfare in funding a "nationally significant" project to the School of Social Work at West Virginia University was that of "improving" and "strengthening" curriculum at the baccalaureate level of preparation for professional practice in social work. As is well known, the original impetus for the very rapid development of baccalaureate programs leading to the professional practice degree came from Section 707 of the 1967 amendment to the Social Security Act. Social work programs leading to the professional practice degree were quickly developed across the country, while the content of those programs already in existence was deepened and enlarged. This growth was supported by the National Association of Social Workers, which acted in 1969 to admit degree holders from Council on Social Work Education–recognized baccalaureate programs to full membership in the professional association.

Following the demise of Section 707 funds in 1973, funding was provided by Title XX for the development and continued support of baccalaureate programs in social work. By 1975, federal funds had made it possible for thousands of undergraduates in hundreds of institutions to enroll in a course of study leading to a professional practice degree in social work. However, by 1975, concern by staff of the Social and Rehabilitation Service had shifted from increasing the number of programs to increasing the quality and stability of programs. A concern emerged as to whether the programs were delivering to the service structure a practitioner prepared with the needed skills, while economic retrenchment brought anxiety that there would not be jobs for all the graduates of baccalaureate level social work programs. In addition, the 70s saw the development of a heightened interest in accountability issues. Would the BSW make a significant difference in terms of improved service delivery? A large investment in development had been made, and now the federal structure was anxious to invest part of its resources in the stabilization, improvement, and refinement of curricula.

The development of the standards for the accreditation of baccalaureate programs in 1973, followed by the implementation of accreditation by the Council on Social Work Education in 1974, indicated the ongoing activities in this direction. By the time the curriculum project was funded, in June 1975, over 200 baccalaureate social work programs had been reviewed by the Commission on Accreditation. One hundred and thirty-five were initially accredited for a varying length of time up to a five year maximum, and seven others were placed in candidacy. This represented a turndown rate of about 30 percent. These initial reviews provided rich insights and information about the content of curricula at the undergraduate level. For the first time, many programs were reviewed in depth against common standards. The West Virginia Curriculum Development Project was funded at the end of the first year of the implementation of accreditation procedures.

While the project was funded with the objective of improving baccalaureate curricula, specifically how this would or could be done was left to the project staff. Following consultation with the executive director and other staff of the Council on Social Work Education, it was concluded that the project must focus on the objectives for entry level professional practice in social work. After determining these objectives, the basic knowledge and skills necessary to achieve them could be defined. While the accreditation standards specify that educational objectives, or anticipated outcomes, of the educational program must be explicated, the specific selection of objectives is left up to each individual program. The standards, which deal only with the level of minimal compliance, do provide some direction. For example, it is stated that students should have "a breadth of learning opportunities designed to familiarize the student with a variety of interventive modes."[1] However, there is considerable variance among programs in specifying educational objectives (see Chapter 3). A similar situation exists with curriculum content. Given the variance in the specification of outcomes, it naturally follows that there would be variance in the emphasis given to content areas.

So long as this situation exists, there can be no assurance to the practice community and the employing agencies that all baccalaureate entry level professional practitioners share a common body of skills. Nor can there be assurance to the next level of social work education, namely, graduate education, that all graduates of baccalaureate programs bring with them common basic knowledge and skills upon which advanced education can be built. For these reasons, the determination was made that the way to improve and strengthen baccalaureate level education would be to attempt to further explicate the objectives and basic content for all baccalaureate programs.

A number of events occurring at the time this project was funded also contributed to the decision to pursue the further definition of the basics for entry level practice. The board of directors of the Council on Social Work Education, in responding to the recommendations of the Task Force Report on Structure and Quality, unanimously passed a recommendation as follows:

Core Content—Immediate attention should be given by the appropriate CSWE unit to further explication of the core content of professional social work education, such content to be inclusive of the knowledge necessary from the basic supporting disciplines, the professional knowledge to be provided as part of the social work education program, and skills to be evidenced in the social work education program.[2]

This action was taken in January 1975 and was subsequently approved by the house of delegates at its spring meeting of that same year.

In its official response to the recommendation of the CSWE Task Force, the National Association of Social Workers responded similarly:

The CSWE Task Forces, individual educators, and many practitioners around the country have expended energy and time trying to categorize the set of knowledge, skills, and values essential to all professional social workers. The terms variously applied to these elements have been "core" and "basic." Perhaps greater clarity will result from the use of the term "fundamental." Thus, when referring to the elements that are taught to all beginning professionals, the professional should be pointing to social work *fundamentals*. When discussing the knowledge and skills that all social workers have in common, we should be talking about the *funda-*

mentals of social work. When we seek to identify the base on which specializations in practice and education are built, the search should lead to the fundamentals. In short, a professional with a bachelor's degree must know and be able to apply these fundamentals. . . .[3]

Later on in the official position statement, NASW emphasized the need for the fundamentals to be "specified fully," so that "the essential content taught in Denver is as consistent as possible with that taught in New York and Portland."[4] Following the action of the house of delegates of the Council on Social Work Education, a subcommittee of the newly formed CSWE Commission on Educational Planning was developed in order to carry out the house mandate to explicate the "base." This subcommittee was already organized when the curriculum project was funded to the School of Social Work at West Virginia University. Project staff, CSWE staff, and leadership of the council mutually agreed that the resources available to the project for purposes of strengthening baccalaureate curricula should, to the fullest extent possible, contribute to the work of the Commission on Educational Planning in explicating the base. This cooperation would be of benefit to the whole of social work education. It was agreed that, in working with the project, the Council on Social Work Education would participate in a formal way, providing consultation and critique, but in no way bound to the project findings.

Hopefully, the project will contribute to the strengthening of baccalaureate programs through developing material that could potentially be utilized to further elaborate and refine current accreditation standards. However, policy issues exist related to the base issue that are beyond the scope and charge given to the project. Such issues as whether or not the project findings constitute a common base for the whole of social work education, or the potential implications for advanced education in social work, were consistently rejected by the project staff as areas inappropriate for project deliberation and concern. Planning and policymaking for the whole of social work education is the responsibility of the Council on Social Work Education, not this project. Nevertheless, in fulfilling its charge to the fullest extent possible, the project may make a contribution to the Council on Social Work Education and, through it, to the entire field of social work education and practice.

Project Methods and Process
The principal methodological operations, and the process of the study from the project's original conception to the writing of this

report, are described in this section. Briefly, the steps were: (1) review of approaches utilized in other curriculum studies; (2) identification of major principles that would guide the project's work; and (3) selection and implementation of a plan and structure that would achieve the project objectives. This last point includes: (1) recruitment and utilization of curriculum consultants; (2) formation and utilization of a Project Advisory Task Force; (3) development of a consultant arrangement with the Council on Social Work Education; (4) development of a liaison and linkage with the National Association of Social Workers and the American Public Welfare Association; (5) organization of workshops with representatives of such special groups as public welfare agencies, national voluntary and federal agencies, social work educators, and BSW practitioners.

In the course of carrying out these activities, the following plan for the project report emerged: (1) statement of project assumptions; (2) development of practice perspectives material, or issues of concern to practitioners; (3) development of objectives, functions and activities for entry level, professional practice in social work; (4) development of competencies for the educational preparation of the baccalaureate social worker; (5) development of knowledge and skills fundamental to the attainment of the competencies for entry level professional practice in social work; (6) identification of special areas for elaboration in position papers; and (7) ongoing review and critique of project materials by task force members, educators and practitioners, and others recognized as experts in the field. Each of these areas will be discussed in some detail in the section that follows. While the presentation is made in a sequential order, the actual implementation of the curriculum development plan was much less strictly ordered.

Review of Approaches Utilized in Other Curriculum Studies

This particular project is not the first effort made to deal with such problems as: What must social workers be able to do? What should be the objectives of the baccalaureate curriculum and what content should be included? This project is merely the most recent attempt to deal with at least some of these issues. Even though the work of the project, unlike that of many other studies, is confined to the entry level of professional educational preparation, the processes and methods utilized by other studies constitute a very rich literature that was helpful in developing the approach utilized in the current curriculum development activity. In reviewing the approaches used by other major studies, particular attention was paid to study design, including the roles of both practitioners and educators in the study process. Staff were also interested in the manner in which educational objectives were formulated and in what kinds of data were secured and utilized to reflect what practitioners would be expected to do. This was based on the presumption that the end result of professional curricula is the development of practitioners who have the skills deemed essential for competent social work practice.

Hollis-Taylor Study of Social Work Education. The first major study of social work education to be reviewed here that explicitly grappled with more effective ways of educating competent social work practitioners was published by Ernest Hollis and Alice Taylor, both employees of federal agencies, in 1951. Hollis was chief of college administration, Office of Education, while Taylor was a training consultant with the Bureau of Public Assistance. The study was sponsored by the National Council on Social Work Education, which had been formed in 1946, to meet the ". . . . immediate pressing problem . . . (of) . . . the need to define more clearly the objectives and content of social work education on the undergraduate and graduate levels."[5] While not a curriculum study, the Hollis-Taylor study did deal with such curriculum areas as objectives, content, and methods as they served to illustrate specific educational proposals. The report establishes "a tentative framework for use in deciding what social work *is* and what it *is not*, all for use in appraising the educational implications of the nature, scope, status, and trends of social work."[6] The report linked education and practice and suggested that an analysis of professional practice tasks is essential to curriculum design. Hollis and Taylor proposed input from practitioners in the form of job analysis as the primary strategy for designing professional social work curricula, with practitioners and educators working together in the development of educational content.

Two committees served in an advisory capacity to the study's staff. The first, the Study Committee, was appointed by the National Council on Social Work Education and had as its primary function counseling the staff on professional and technical matters. It consisted of six educators and one practitioner who was employed by the Federal Security Agency. The second committee, the National Advisory Committee, was selected by Dr. Hollis to "Help him relate education for social workers to the rest of the intellectual administrative fabric of higher education, and to the realities of social welfare as they are seen by citizens who are laymen in the field of social work."[7] This committee, comprised of twenty individuals, included college presidents, the commissioner of the Federal Security Agency, and several of the top leadership of national voluntary agencies. Neither of these committees was asked to endorse the final report or to subscribe to its conclusions and recommendations. Thus, the final report emerged as a staff document.

Council on Social Work Education Curriculum Study—1959. The Hollis and Taylor study was followed by the most extensive social work curriculum study ever undertaken. This study, published in 1959, was commissioned by the Council on Social Work Education and was conducted under the leadership of Werner Boehm, assisted by a number of social work educators. A threefold question was addressed: "What are the desirable educational objectives for social work education, into what curriculum areas should they be organized, and what should be their distribution over the undergraduate-graduate continuum?"[8] Along with the social work educators who directed the several areas of this study, a "Technical Advisory Panel" for the total study was created. This group of twenty-one included fifteen persons from education and six from practice areas. Each of the various study areas[9] was conducted with the assistance of an "Advisory Panel" created in order to provide the opportunity for each project director "to test the direction in which his analysis was moving against the judgment of a group of experts."[10]

In the Boehm volume summarizing the findings and recommendations of this study, the link between practice and education appears to have been weakened by shifting the input into curriculum development from equal participation by practitioners and educators to dominance by educators. This summary document minimized task analysis and practitioner input as strategies for curriculum development, although both were included in some of the specialized volumes, such as the one concerning the public social services. However, the study of undergraduate education, directed by Herbert Bisno, serves well to illustrate the heavy reliance on educators. The undergraduate study, a landmark in the history of baccalaureate education, focused on the question: "What should be the function, content and organization of undergraduate education and of the training of social workers?"[11] Interestingly, the study dealt little with what baccalaureate level practitioners should be prepared to *do*, but instead went to the question: "What are desirable objectives for the undergraduate phase of the program of social work education?"[12] The objectives were arrived at through "some ideas which came from persons conferred with on the field trip. The literature of social work also was helpful. But in this aspect of the study, the most important resource was the course materials received from schools."[13] Finally, the advisory panel to the undergraduate study included nineteen persons, of whom fifteen were educators. Thus, in the CSWE curriculum study, the overriding strategy for professional social work curriculum design became the study of existing curriculum and the use of ideas from social work educators as to what curriculum content ought to be.

Madison Study. The CSWE Curriculum Study was followed almost immediately by a study of undergraduate social work education by Bernice Madison which was supported by the Rosenberg Foundation and published in 1960. The ultimate goal of this study was to "propose an undergraduate social welfare curriculum, conceived in the liberal arts tradition and educationally sound, which will prepare students for graduate study in social work and for fulfilling certain functions of the welfare field. In relation to the latter, this curriculum is designed to educate students for performing at an initial level of competence in a generic discipline, not in a specific setting."[14]

It appears that Madison, too, was searching for a basic curriculum, but one that would be responsive to the demands of practice in the public agency. Thus, a meticulous analysis of what workers in public assistance were actually doing was carried out. Then, based on this task analysis data, the study determined which job activities could be carried out successfully by graduates from baccalaureate programs in social welfare. A panel of "competent social work practitioners and educators" (equally represented) made judgments concerning the appropriateness of the empirical data for integration into educational objectives. In addition to the task analysis data, consistency with the mission of the profession and with sound educational principles were also utilized as "screens" in the formulation of educational objectives. Madison emphasized that "curricula ought not to prepare students only for what is currently expected in jobs."[15]

Madison's study very strongly links practice to education and equally strongly looks to practice activities as the base for curriculum development. The overriding curriculum development strategy represented by this study is the use of task analysis to generate curriculum objectives and content.

Syracuse University–Veterans Administration Project—1972. In the spring of 1969, the Syracuse University School of Social Work received a grant from the U.S. Veterans Administration to conduct a project on manpower research in undergraduate social work curriculum building. This project, directed by Lester J. Glick and Thomas Briggs, sought to bring together existing empirical data related to the utilization and abilities of baccalaureate level social workers. The empirical data were obtained from the findings of major research and demonstration projects conducted or concluded between the period 1965-1970 on social work manpower utilization.[16] The purpose of the research was to gather existing information, which was then made available to the curriculum planners. Ten major findings relevant to the utilization and abilities of the BSW were distilled from the review of the major research and demonstration projects,[17] all of which have implications for curriculum building and, presumably, were utilized by the fifteen social work curriculum planners who worked together in task forces in an effort to "provide greater specificity for undergraduate social work education."[18] Curriculum implications were developed based on a set of behaviors that the project felt could be expected of baccalaureate level social workers.[19]

This approach to curriculum development emphasized the role of the educator as researcher. Like the Madison study, the Syracuse University-VA project also articulated the need to relate curriculum content to what workers are actually doing in practice. Practitioners participated in the data collection process, but they appear to have had little input into the curriculum planning phase of the project activity.

Southern Regional Education Board Studies. The first of these two studies, *Manpower Utilization in Social Welfare* (1970), attempted to define the appropriate roles and functions for a beginning level professional social worker. Harold MacPheeters, the director of the project, and Robert Teare, consultant to the project, used a more expanded task analysis approach than that used by Madison, one that they spoke of in terms of "formulating and configuring job activities." They distinguished between two aspects of task analysis: job factoring and developmental analysis. Job factoring is "breaking down jobs into tasks clustered together on the basis of skill requirements of difficulty," while developmental analysis "starts with analysis of the needs of the public and the profession and then proceeds to the definition of tasks designed to meet these needs."[20]

The manpower utilization project provided a framework for a rational model of the baccalaureate worker in relation to other levels of workers. It did not attempt to identify the specific competencies of the baccalaureate worker; that task was attempted by the core of competence project which followed. In launching this project, MacPheeters emphasized that "there seems to be a need for some consistent core of competence that can be expected for any [BSW] . . . a core upon which job descriptions, merit examinations and certification or licensure could be based."[21] In order to arrive at the "core of competence," the project invited fifteen persons to participate in working conferences. Building upon the roles and functions developed by the earlier manpower utilization project, participants identified the knowledge, skills, and values that were felt to be essential to carrying out the functions of each of the roles. Judgments were made about whether the items of knowledge, values, and skills were "virtually essential, highly desirable, or optional" for a baccalaureate level worker. All but four of the seventeen persons who served on the core of competence task force were educators, while in the earlier manpower utilization project, the project staff and a core group of faculty persons worked with representatives of "consumers of social welfare services, personnel systems, and the Federal Government" to identify people's needs and to determine what functions should be carried out to meet those needs.[22] Even so, it appears that in both SREB projects, educators tended to carry the dominant role.

The Selection of a Curriculum Development Approach for this Project

This type of brief overview cannot do justice to all the ongoing attempts to deal with developing curricula for educating competent social workers, especially at the undergraduate level. Nevertheless, it is sufficient to identify three major curriculum development strategies that were helpful to this project in developing its particular approach.

1. A primary focus on input from practitioners to identify the tasks that competent social workers perform and for which students in professional social work curricula must be prepared. This approach appears to be based on three assumptions: (a) social work education is education for practice; (b) there must be a close relationship between what social work practitioners do and their education; and (c) social work practitioners should have substantial input into curriculum content, although not primary responsibility for it. This approach tends to maximize cooperation between educators and practitioners in the educational process.

2. A primary focus on input from educators to identify the content

that best prepares a competent practitioner. This approach leaves the definition of what constitutes competent practice to educators who may use one or more of the following in this process: research findings; peer consultation; social science, education, or other relevant theory; or other sources of data. Links between education and practice can become very weak in this approach.

3. A primary focus on input from the results of task analysis in which curriculum is built to reflect what practitioners actually do, what various relevant groups think they ought to do, or some combination of both. This approach tends to have strong links between education and practice but can limit the input of educators if the relationship of their input to practice is not immediately obvious.

This project adopted a curriculum development strategy that placed primary emphasis on the first approach, with elements of the second and third approaches present. More specifically, certain principles emerged and served to guide the curriculum development activity.

1. The charge to the project, to further explicate objectives and basic content for the entry level of practice in social work, mandates the involvement of all of the major systems involved. The issue and how it is resolved will affect the organized profession, social work education, practitioners and employing agencies, students and consumer groups, as well as social work educators. Since all are affected, all ought to be involved to the maximum extent feasible and possible.

2. Specific educational objectives for the preparation of the entry level practitioner and basic curriculum content can be developed only if there is some greater clarity and agreement as to what the entry level practitioner ought to be prepared to *do*. The project should, therefore, strive for clarity and consensus among the major groups and individuals involved in the definition of the purposes of social work practice.

3. The project should function in a climate of openness. Contributions, suggestions, and criticism should be invited at all points in the project's work so that there is an ongoing process of feedback and modification.

4. Practitioners, either as individuals or representatives of organizations, should be involved as full partners in the endeavor. Neither educators nor practitioners should predominate, although it must be recognized that appropriate roles, interests, and contributions differ.

5. Curriculum content should flow from the anticipated practice outcomes, rather than from any preconceived notions regarding past and current curriculum content.
6. The project should recognize and accept that it is simply another step in ongoing, long-term efforts to further define the basics for social work practice. In this sense, participants in the activity of the project should view the project's work as contributing to this process, rather than being final or definitive.

THE WORKING STRUCTURE OF THE PROJECT

With these principles in mind, we turn now to a description of the structure created to attain project objectives. This will include a description of the activities undertaken by each subpart of the project structure as they relate to attainment of the objectives.

The Project Task Force

The Project Task Force, formed during the early months of the first grant period, was made up of social work educators and social work practitioners. Two were appointed by the National Association of Social Workers as liaison between that organization and the project, and other individuals represented the American Public Welfare Association. The task force held three formal meetings during the period 1975-1977. However, individual members of the task force participated in and assisted with the coordination of workshops held (see below). Task force members also participated in other professional meetings and conferences, so that there was ongoing and frequent contact with the membership.

Through its discussions of practice and curriculum issues, the task force provided substantial input to project documents. It also reviewed drafts of all documents, providing critiques and making suggestions for revisions.

Project Consultants

Throughout its life, the project drew upon a select group of educators who served as consultants. During the first year, educators on the task force served as well in special consultative roles. They discussed issues in depth and drafted position statements in many of these areas. During the second year, they continued, as members of the task force, to provide special counsel and assistance, while other social work educators, including representatives of major ethnic and minority groups, provided consultation to the project on an ad hoc basis.

Project Staff

In order to insure consistent direction and to maintain momentum, the project director was relieved of other assignments at the School of Social Work, West Virginia University, and assigned on a full-time basis to the project. During the second year of the project, a second full-time project associate was employed. Dr. Frank M. Loewenberg, formerly of the Council on Social Work Education staff, joined the project staff during the summer months of 1976.

In addition to initiating and coordinating project activities, project staff did extensive research for, writing, and preparation of the final drafts of project documents. The staff maintained ongoing formal and informal contacts with the profession and did the preparation necessary to relate project activities to contemporary trends in higher education.

Council on Social Work Education
Consultation to the Project

During both years of the project's work, consultation was secured from the Council on Social Work Education through subcontract. Dr. Miriam Dinerman was employed by the CSWE and provided the consultation service for the 1975–1976 grant period; Dr. Ralph Dolgoff served in this capacity throughout the second year.

Workshops

Five special workshops were held during the first year of the project for purposes of (1) identifying issues and concerns of practitioners and their relevance for curriculum planning and development; (2) securing reactions from educators and practitioners to the project and its initial positions; and (3) sensitizing project staff and curriculum consultants to practice needs and issues as these were perceived by participants* in the workshops. The *workshops* were

1. American Public Welfare Association—The project co-sponsored a workshop with a group of public welfare personnel representing the range of levels of practice within the public welfare agency.
2. National Association of Social Workers—The project co-sponsored a workshop to which persons representing the professional association were invited.
3. National voluntary and federal agency representatives—A range of individuals representing these agencies, many of whom were in personnel utilization, as well as planning and policymaking positions, participated in this workshop.

*For a full listing of participants, see Appendix C.

4. Council on Social Work Education—The project co-sponsored a workshop with a selected group of educators, including persons chairing or serving on commissions of the council.
5. Association of Baccalaureate Social Workers—The project co-sponsored a workshop to which two BSW practitioners from each of the ten HEW regions were invited. In selecting this group, all of whom were graduates of CSWE-accredited programs, an effort was made to involve individuals who represented a broad range of practice settings.

From these workshops, certain consistent themes emerged that were felt to have strong significance for curriculum planning. These were developed in a paper entitled "Practice Perspectives Related to Social Work Education" which is included in Chapter 5. It should be noted here that in most instances, participants to the workshops represented themselves rather than the whole of practice. However, most of the positions held and issues raised were also confirmed and supported by the recent CSWE Task Force report on Practice and Education.

Finally, the workshops served to identify some areas that, in the judgment of project staff, needed further and more specific elaboration. These areas, for which special papers were commissioned, included Professional Values and Professional Ethics in Social Work Education, Educational Milieu as Curriculum, Bureaucratic Functioning as a Social Work Skill, and Social Work in Governmental Agencies. A fifth area, dealing with preparation for practice with members of diverse groups, is deemed to be critical by the project. However, an appropriate paper could not be developed given the time and other resources available. The papers were not intended to be definitive, but rather to raise issues relevant to social work education in each area.

THE USE OF THE PROJECT STRUCTURE
TO CREATE THE PROJECT REPORT

The above described structure and activities have been brought together and organized in this report. Three sections of the report are briefly described below, focusing on the way in which the project's structure contributed to the development of each section. These sections are those most directly related to the identification of appropriate practice expectations for entry level professional social workers and the curriculum content fundamental to the education of persons to meet these expectations.

Project Assumptions[23]

Very early in the life of the project, work was begun on the development of a series of "assumptions," which have been revised and modified throughout the life of the project. These assumptions aim to articulate the point of view that would form the basis, both pragmatically and philosophically, for the subsequent curriculum development activites. In formulating this piece of the project's work, it became clear that certain of the assumptions were readily accepted because action and/or broad consensus had already been achieved within the profession. Consensus within the profession and social work education does not exist on other of the assumptions, however, and a high degree of acceptance by the curriculum consultants from within the task force was achieved only after lengthy discussion and debate. The project could not carry out its mission unless it took a position with regard to specific issues related to the nature of social work practice and education. These positions are stated in the assumptions.

Development of Objectives, Functions, and
Activities for Entry Level Professional
Practice in Social Work

No other area created as much frustration and difficulty for the project as did the development of this material. For the first several months of the project, an effort was made to develop objectives and content for entry level professional practice in social work without the specific delineation of what the entry level practitioner might be expected to do. "Laundry lists" began to emerge. Following the second meeting of the task force, in September 1976, project staff were urged to define with as much clarity as possible the activities deemed appropriate for the entry level professional practitioner. This was consistent with the thrust of the project toward developing curriculum content from anticipated practice outcomes.

The project developed a statement of objectives, functions and activities for entry level, professional practice in social work by drawing upon a variety of materials and activities: the Florida Task Bank, a comprehensive study that examined the tasks actually being carried out by a range of workers in public agency settings; other task analysis work available to the project; the work of the Chicago Community Fund, a study of job descriptions for workers in a range of private agencies; the Syracuse University Veterans Administration Project; the work of the Southern Regional Education Board in defining a "core of competence" for the baccalaureate social worker; contributions from practitioners in the project-sponsored workshops held during the first year of the project; the project's Advisory Task Force; the literature in the field; and a broad range of educators with whom the project had contact. Throughout the development of the material, project staff engaged in testing its content with groups of educators and practitioners.

Finally, the material was submitted to several groups for their formal review. These groups included selected educators representing official bodies of the Council on Social Work Education, including the Commissions on Accreditation, Educational Policy and Planning, Minorities, and Women, as well as educators selected for their acknowledged expertness in curriculum conceptualization; the National Association of Social Workers' Task Force on the Baccalaureate Social Worker in the Profession; official representatives of the National Association of Social Workers; and both staff members of the American Public Welfare Association and individuals representing practice in the public agency. These groups served as panels to review the material and to flag activities that substantial numbers of the participants deemed as wholly inappropriate for the entry level worker. In addition, areas of omission were noted. Following revisions, the material was submitted to the Project Advisory Task Force for final review.

All of the functions and activities had to be consistent with the project's defintion of social work. Activities drawn from task analysis material and definitions of what workers ought to be doing were put in the context of the purposes of social work. It should be noted that some persons differed with the project's definition of social work. In any event, the final document does reflect a high degree of consensus by the groups that reviewed the material.

Development of Statement of Competencies for the Educational Preparation of the Baccalaureate Social Worker

The objectives, functions, and activities material was utilized to develop a statement of competencies for the educational preparation of the entry level social worker. The project decided to adopt a competency approach from which the knowledge, values, and skills would be explicated. Some rationale for this may be helpful.

The approach is described as follows by Robert Houston:

> From these two perceived needs—accountability and personalization— has come the movement referred to as competency-based . . . education. . . . Advocates of [competency-based education] . . . refer to the way in which the learner demonstrates knowledge and skills. . . . The

emphasis on performance reminds us that knowledge alone is inadequate; knowledge must be employed in overt action.[24]

Although it is a relatively recent educational approach, competency-based learning[25] has its roots in the educational theories of Ralph Tyler, which have strongly influenced higher education, including social work education, for many years. Madison summarizes his work as follows:

> It involves: (a) Deciding upon educational objectives and expressing them in a form helpful in selecting learning experiences and guiding teaching; (b) Choosing and creating learning experiences through which the student will attain the objectives decided upon; (c) Organizing the learning experiences for effective instruction in line with the criteria of continuity, sequence, and integration; (d) Evaluation.[26]

Obviously, Tyler's work relates closely to the need to be able to specify what the baccalaureate social work practitioner must be competent to do to carry out the activities appropriate for his level of professional practice. Without such specification, the setting of curriculum objectives and the selection of content and teaching-learning experiences are impossible. Tyler also emphasizes that learning must include knowledge, value, and skill components.

An important aspect of competency-based learning is the evaluation of competency mastery. This is one of the approach's important contributions to social work education, since it provides a mechanism for insuring that the graduate of a social work education program has in fact mastered the educational content. At this point in the project's progress, it is premature to develop evaluative tools, but the project recognizes this as an important priority for the future.

Defining educational outcomes in terms of competencies has a number of advantages for baccalaureate level professional social work education. Three are of particular importance.

1. *Compatibility with the current societal environment in which higher education exists.* Davies has summarized this environment as follows:

> Education and training represents the largest single national expenditure, and many economists and politicians now believe that it is doubtful if society can any longer afford the high cost and low productivity associated with education. In the past, we have, to a very large extent, been concerned with teaching rather than learning, with the means rather than the ends of education. The last decade, however, has witnessed . . . an increasing concern with an emphasis upon the achievement of educational goals and objectives.[27]

The increasing demand for accountability requires that all higher education, including social work, be more concerned with whether education is effectively doing what it says it is doing. This includes baccalaureate professional social work education that claims to educate effective practitioners. Unless it can demonstrate that its graduates are competent in the performance of their professional tasks, the basis for professional autonomy will be seriously eroded.

2. *Educating an increasingly diverse student population.* Given social work's historic and continuing commitment to persons from different socioeconomic, ethnic, racial, and lifestyle backgrounds, the curriculum must incorporate content on human diversity and permit students with widely different knowledge and learning backgrounds to use their existing knowledge and to build upon it. The curriculum should also be amenable to flexible structural patterns, since many students have to work while they study. In a society characterized by rapid occupational shifts and by the reentry of older students into programs of study after raising families or when retraining becomes necessary, the curriculum should be adaptable to adult learners with a rich life experience background. It must also enable the student seeking a second degree to proceed with minimal waste of his or her previous learning experiences, including activities such as reading, films, role-play, observation, research activities, and community involvement. This would lead to the mastery of that content by allowing students flexibility in learning opportunities rather than confing them to only one type of educational activity, which may be ineffective for them. The student is also allowed to proceed at his or her own pace, studying until competency is attained. This removes the student from a time-limited educational experience, which may be inadequate for competency attainment, as well as allowing the student already having competency in a content area to move on to areas in which further learning is needed. These characteristics of a competency approach allow students to make maximum use of their learning abilities and existing competencies, regardless of the nature of their prior educational background and their life experiences.

3. *Communicating effectively with practitioners.* In a practice profession like social work, it is important that educators and practitioners be able to communicate effectively. This is necessary if practitioners are to have ongoing input into social work education and if practitioners, as potential employers of graduates, are to have realistic expectations when hiring baccalaureate social workers. Effective communication is facilitated by educational outcomes which are stated in terms of practice competencies.

Project staff developed knowledge and skill elements from each of the competencies. Obviously, there was redundancy, since practically all of the competencies include some similar knowledge and skill components. In order to eliminate redundancy, the knowledge and skill components were then categorized for presentation purposes.

SUMMARY

Finally, it needs to be reemphasized that the work of this project is another step in a process of long duration. Although it builds on the richness of earlier studies, it is the first major curriculum development project to occur after undergraduate social work education was given the mandate by NASW and CSWE to educate entry level professional practitioners. This project's major objectives, then, were to develop curriculum content that would facilitate the attainment of entry level practice competencies as they are defined by the project. In working toward these objectives, the project has utilized contributions from practitioners, educators, representatives of professional organizations, consultants, and project staff.

NOTES

1. "Standards for the Accreditation of Baccalaureate Social Work Programs" (New York: Council on Social Work Education, July 1, 1974).
2. "Summary of Discussion and Action by Board of Directors at its meeting of January 20-21" (New York: Council on Social Work Education, 1975).
3. "Official Position on Recommendations of Council on Social Work Education Task Force on Structure and Quality in Social Work Education and Task Force on Practice and Education" (New York: Council on Social Work Education, October 1975), p. 4.
4. Ibid., p. 7.
5. Hollis, Ernest, and Alice Taylor, *Social Work Education in the United States* (New York: Columbia University Press, 1951), p. ii.
6. Ibid., p. xi.
7. Ibid., p. xiii.
8. Boehm, Werner. *Objectives of the Social Work Curriculum of the Future* (New York: Council on Social Work Education, 1959), p. 21.
9. Study areas included Undergraduate, Administration, Community Organization, Corrections, Human Growth and Behavior, Public Social Services, Rehabilitation, Research, Casework, Group Work, Social Welfare Policy and Services, Values and Ethics.
10. Boehm, p. 31.
11. Bisno, Herbert. *The Place of the Undergraduate Curriculum in Social Work Education* (New York: Council on Social Work Education, 1959), p. 3.
12. Ibid., p. 104.

13. Ibid., p. 104.

14. Madison, Bernice, *Undergraduate Education for Social Welfare* (San Francisco: Rosenberg Foundation, 1960), p. 1.

15. Ibid., p. 3.

16. Barker, Robert, and Thomas Briggs, eds., *Manpower Research on the Utilization of Baccalaureate Social Workers: Implications for Education* (Washington, D.C., United States Government Printing Office, 1972), p. 4.

17. Ibid., pp. 90–95.

18. Glick, Lester, ed., *Undergraduate Social Work Education for Practice: A Report on Curriculum Content and Issues* (Washington, D.C.: United States Government Printing Office, 1972), p. 1.

19. Barker and Briggs, pp. 104–105.

20. Teare, Robert, and Harold MacPheeters, *Manpower Utilization in Social Welfare* (Atlanta: Southern Regional Education Board, 1970), p. 4.

21. Ryan, Robert, and Harold MacPheeters, *A Core of Competence for Baccalaureate Social Welfare* (Atlanta: Southern Regional Educational Board, 1971), p. 29.

22. Ibid., pp. 11–12.

23. The term is used here to denote a statement accepted as true, even though without proof.

24. Houston, W. Robert, ed., *Exploring Competency Based Education* (Berkeley: McCutchan Publishing, 1974), p. 7.

25. Competency-based learning can be distinguished from the educational technology called competency-based education, which has a clearly defined set of teaching-learning procedures. This project has not adopted a strict competency-based educational technology (although of course individual schools may wish to). It has adopted features of competency-based learning however, most of which have already been discussed; clear specification of curriculum, learning, and performance objectives; the belief that curriculum content must be directly related to practice competency; the organization of curriculum content as flexibly as possible so that already existing competencies are recognized and further developed in a logical, sequential manner; and the belief that curriculum content must include competency in knowledge mastery, skill performance, and value integration.

26. Madison, p. 14.

27. Davies, Ivor, *Competency Based Learning: Technology, Management, and Design* (New York: McGraw-Hill, 1973), p. 4.

REFERENCES AND BIBLIOGRAPHY

A Personnel Management Program Guide. Chicago: Community Fund of Chicago, Inc., August 1973.

Abbott, Edith. *Social Welfare and Professional Education.* Rev. ed. Chicago: University of Chicago Press, 1942.

American Association of Schools of Social Work. *Professional Education.* New York, 1948.

"An Analysis of Hiring Requirements for Social Service Classifications in

State Merit Systems." Washington, D.C.: National Association of Social Workers, 1975.

Arkava, Morton L., and E. Clifford Brennan. *Competency-Based Education for Social Work: Evaluation and Curriculum Issues.* New York: Council on Social Work Education, 1976.

Armitage, Andrew, and Frank Clark. "Design Issues in the Performance-Based Curriculum." *Journal of Education for Social Work* 11, 1 (Winter 1975).

Austin, Michael J., and Philip L. Smith. *Florida Human Service Task Bank.* Tallahassee: State University System of Florida, October 1975.

Austin, Michael J., and Philip L. Smith. *Personnel and Staff Development Planning for the Human Services.* Tallahassee: State University System of Florida, October 1975.

Barker, Robert, and Thomas Briggs, eds. *Manpower Research on the Utilization of Baccalaureate Social Workers: Implications for Education.* Washington, D.C., United States Government Printing Office, 1972.

Barlow, Henry, ed. *Higher Education and the Social Professions.* Lexington, Kentucky: College of Social Professions, 1973.

Bisno, Herbert. *The Place of the Undergraduate Curriculum in Social Work Education.* New York: Council on Social Work Education, 1959.

Boehm, Werner. *Objectives of the Social Work Curriculum of the Future.* New York: Council on Social Work Education, 1959.

Brawley, Edward E. *The New Human Service Worker: Community College Education and the Social Services.* New York: Praeger, 1975.

Daly, Dorothy Bird. "Educating the Undergraduate for Professional Social Work Roles." In Barker and Briggs, eds., *Manpower Research on the Utilization of Baccalaureate Social Workers* (Washington, D.C.: United States Government Printing Office, 1972), pp. 97–106.

Davies, Ivor. *Competency Based Learning: Technology, Management, and Design.* New York: McGraw-Hill, 1973.

Dolgoff, Ralph. "Report to the Task Force on Social Work Practice and Education." New York: Council on Social Work Education, August 1974.

Euster, Gerald L. "The Job Market for Undergraduate Social Work Education." *Social Work Education Reporter.* April 1973, pp. 39–43.

Glick, Lester, ed. *Undergraduate Social Work Education for Practice: A Report on Curriculum Content and Issues.* Washington, D.C.: United States Government Printing Office, 1972.

Hollis, Ernest, and Alice Taylor. *Social Work Education in the United States.* New York: Columbia University Press, 1951.

Houston, W. Robert, ed. *Exploring Competency Based Education.* Berkeley: McCutchan Publishing, 1974.

Lewis, Robert E. *A Systems Approach to Manpower Utilization and Training.* Salt Lake City: Utah Division of Family Services, October 1972.

Lewis, Robert E.; Richard Brady; and Wayne Pearson. *A Beginning Task Bank For Rural Comprehensive Human Services Delivery System.* Salt Lake City: Utah Department of Social Services, January 1974.

Madison, Bernice. *Undergraduate Education for Social Welfare.* San Francisco: Rosenberg Foundation, 1960.

Middleman, Ruth, and Gale Goldberg. *Social Service Delivery: A Structural*

Approach to Social Work Practice. New York: Columbia University Press, 1974.

"Minimum Competency Profile: BSW Practitioner." Toronto: Ontario Association of Professional Social Workers, November 1975.

O'Connell, William R., and W.E. Moomaw. *A CBC Primer.* Atlanta: Southern Regional Education Board, 1975.

"Official Position on Recommendations of Council on Social Work Education Task Force on Structure and Quality in Social Work Education and Task Force on Practice and Education." New York: Council on Social Work Education, October 1975.

Pincus, Allen, and Anne Minahan. *Social Work Practice: Model and Method.* Itaca, Illinois: F.E. Peacock Publishers, 1973.

Pins, Arnulf. *An Overview of Undergraduate Education in Social Welfare.* New York: Council on Social Work Education, 1968.

Report of the National Curriculum Workshop. (Allerton, Illinois). *Building the Social Work Curriculum.* New York: Council on Social Work Education, 1961.

Ryan, Robert, and Harold MacPheeters. *A Core of Competence for Baccalaureate Social Welfare.* Atlanta: Southern Regional Education Board, 1971.

Siporin, Max. *Introduction to Social Work Practice.* New York: MacMillan Publishing Company, Inc., 1975.

"Standards for the Accreditation of Baccalaureate Social Work Programs." New York: Council on Social Work Education, July 1, 1974.

"Summary of Discussion and Action by Board of Directors at its Meeting of January 20–21, 1975." New York: Council on Social Work Education.

Teare, Robert, and Harold MacPheeters. *Manpower Utilization in Social Welfare.* Atlanta: Southern Regional Education Board, 1970.

Volmer, William S. *Final Report on the Workstandards Task Force for Social Services and Income Maintenance.* Baltimore, Maryland: Social Services Administration, January 1976.

Walker, Sydnor. *Social Work and the Training of Social Workers.* Chapel Hill: University of North Carolina Press, 1928.

Wexler, Murray. "The Behavioral Sciences in Medical Education: A View from Psychology." *American Psychologist,* April 1976, pp. 275–83.

Youngdahl, Benjamin. "Shall We Face It?" In American Association of Schools of Social Work, *Professional Education* (New York, 1948), pp. 31–38.

 *Chapter 5*

Practice Perspectives Related to
Social Work Education

INTRODUCTION

Some 125 individuals attended and participated in workshops co-sponsored by the project during 1975–1976 grant
period. These workshops, described in great detail in Chapter 4, were
held for the purpose of securing practitioner reaction to initial project positions and of getting ideas and suggestions from practitioners
regarding what they thought entry level professional social workers
ought to be prepared to do. In the course of the workshop sessions,
it was natural that participants would reflect upon and criticize their
own educational experiences as well as those of recent graduates with
whom they have interacted.

Participants to the workshops were selected in various ways
depending upon the organizational co-sponsor with the project. The
leadership of the American Public Welfare Association developed the
list of participants invited to that workshop. In doing so, they gave
recognition to the range of levels of workers within the public
agency. The participants at the workship co-sponsored by the National Association of Social Workers were selected by the NASW.
Persons were invited to participate in the meeting with representatives of national voluntary and federal agencies according to their
position within their particular agency. The BSW practitioner workshop was attended by two BSW practitioners from each of the ten
HEW regions. The participants at this workshop were selected from
a list of practitioners, all of whom were graduated from accredited
programs, developed by the project in cooperation with the Associa-

tion of Baccalaureate Social Work Program Directors. An effort was made to secure as much diversity among the participants as possible in terms of practice setting, worker assignments, race and ethnicity, length of time in position, and program from which the participant was graduated (small liberal arts institution, program in School of Social Work, etc.). Finally, the project director had the opportunity to meet with a group of foster parents representing the National Foster Parent Association. The comments of these individuals, as they reflected on the kinds of expectations they had of their social workers, were most helpful.

As has been noted elsewhere in this report, it must be understood that the information secured from practice participants cannot be presented as reflective of the whole of the practice or service communities. However, the material has, from the point of view of the project staff and the Advisory Task Force, rich implications for curriculum development. In addition, the serious deliberations of all participants were never significantly at odds with earlier practitioner reflections on the content of curricula of educational programs, most notably the CSWE Task Force Report on Practice and Education.

One additional new dimension was added, however. Insofar as the project staff are aware, the BSW practitioner workshop was the first national meeting held with BSWs from across the country for the purpose of assessing their educational preparedness in relation to entry job expectations. Given the lack of coherence in the utilization of entry level practitioners, the extent of agreement on many issues on the part of BSW participants was somewhat surprising.

In the sections that follow, Jacqueline D. Fassett, NASW liaison to the project and now first vice president of NASW, comments on overall practice concerns and issues as she perceived them from the workshops. Her remarks are followed by a summarization by project staff of the issues raised by the BSW practitioners who participated in the workshop held to specifically seek their contributions.

OVERALL PRACTICE CONCERNS
AND ISSUES
Jacqueline D. Fassett, LCSW,
Practice Consultant

In very specific terms, the outcomes of the social work education process are the practice competencies of persons entering the profession. This has been the consistent posture of practitioners. The same concerns that have been addressed by the profession as a whole have been directed toward social work education—preoccupation with process and neglect of outcome issues. The West Virginia Undergraduate Curriculum Development Project was designed to correct the imbalance. A major input component has come from all levels of the practice community, assuring the presentation of a comprehensive, diversified statement of what agencies expect in the entry level worker.

An almost infinite range of practice skills and competencies is reflected in the delivery of social work services. This observation is implicit if we accept the wide-ranging activities and responsibilities reflected in what social workers are actually doing in order to serve populations in need. Obviously there are conflicting opinions as to whether or not all of these functions can be identified as legitimate professional activities. Social workers who rigidly hold to limited perceptions of social work practice might very well reject efforts to meet concrete needs as bonafide professional functions. These same social workers also reject the legitimacy of the BSW practitioner, despite the fact that this entry level has been legitimized and supported by actions taken by NASW and CSWE.

Within this framework, we will attempt to identify basic curriculum content needs from the practice perspective. Dominant themes culled from workshops held throughout the country have been integrated in this final document. The practice consultants with the project reflect a wide representation of skills, experience, academic levels, and systems. They have contributed effectively to the project process and are satisfied that the outcome will be indicative of what the field of practice needs and wants in the entry level BSW practitioner.

The primary practice arenas for beginning social workers are the large public systems that reflect legislative and governmental policy decisions. Unfortunately, too many new social workers embark on practice careers with an essentially negative view of these bureaucratic structures. This orientation inhibits systemic understanding and ultimately affects worker ability to utilize systemic supports on behalf of clients in a positive way. We have consistently confronted the lack of preparation during the educational process for a beginning analysis of the service system. Social workers need to be taught about the bureaucratic system components that can be utilized in developing a workable understanding. The agency—its structure, funding, sanctions, and methods of accountability—must be seen in relation to client needs. Such skills are needed to enable new workers to function effectively; with them, one can begin to work effectively in using agency resources to provide appropriate services.

BSW practitioners have identified clearly discrepancies between what they have been taught and what they encounter in practice. The individual system must be seen and understood in relation to the whole social welfare spectrum. Inter- and intrasystem relationships and functioning need to be understood at the formal as well as informal levels. The BSW practitioner must also understand agencies in terms of their politics and power structures. Discovery of these realities without adequate preparation has had devastating effects on many of our new, eager and creative talents. Robert Pruger[1] presents a comprehensive view of how social work functions within bureaucratic structures.

The misperceptions of the dynamics and realities of change suggest another area of need. It is imperative that the beginning worker understand change from a differential perspective. The kinds of change and the degrees of change have very obvious implications for the development of appropriate strategies. The implied expectations that burden new workers because these issues have not been clearly presented have created crippling tensions and frustrations. It is an act of irresponsibility to send new practitioners into the field with the belief that their primary mission is to radically change agency objectives and structure. Untold energies are spent in attempting to reconcile what practitioners view as a conflict between their professional ethical structure and the demands of agencies. Believing that the agency position is antithetical to human service needs, new workers develop a sense of "self hate" from seeing themselves as purveyors of negative factors.

> Graduates need to understand that effecting change in organizations and agencies requires an understanding of how agencies, in general, and the subject one in particular, came to be, what forces support their continued existence and who are the people, within and without the agency, who can bring about change. Change must be planned and a strategy implemented which is realistic and which will not create consequences which are more harmful than the condition to be changed. Students need an opportunity to learn how to participate, with others, in continuing incremental change which will renew agencies to keep them effective in a changing environment.[2]

There is lack of both understanding and agreement on the difference between basic practice competence and the ability to function within the framework of a "generalist" model. Some workshop participants felt that this model implies a level of practice sophistication that is unrealistic for BSW activity and that the ability to apply basic skills and knowledge to specific services and tasks would provide a more comfortable perspective.

Given the apparent range of functions currently assigned to BSW practitioners throughout the country, it is clear that curriculum content cannot be designed to prepare practitioners for specialty functions. Participants suggested that students should be able to work with variety and difference and be trained in the processes involved in learning about new areas quickly. It is not possible for a curriculum to encompass all of the specialty areas, such as health, drugs, aging, in detail. Students need to know the sources of information and the fundamental principles to be applied to new situations. It was noted that "practitioners learn 80% of what they do on the job," suggesting the need for strong cooperative arrangements between schools and practice agencies in developing and coordinating educational programs.

The issue of practice roles and activities provoked wide-ranging responses from workshop participants. A full range of determinants exists in the field, including total absence of structure and narrowly defined job descriptions. Students need to learn and appreciate the freeing aspects of limits and parameters as opposed to viewing constraints from a negative perspective. Understanding and defining agency structure and policies enables the practitioner to deal positively with accountability issues. The ability to assess needs and seek consultation appropriately must grow out of the educational process.

Much attention needs to be given to effective communication skills, both oral and written. Current reality also requires familiarity with budgeting, informational systems, and data technology. With expanded involvement of social workers in the preparation of software for computers, the educational process must incorporate basic understanding of management information systems and of how they relate to the mandates for increased accountability.

Professional socialization was viewed by many participants as a critical component of educational process. The current ambiguities within the social work profession toward BSW practitioners do not support this process. Knowledge of the profession, its values, and its ethical structure are viewed as crucial to the development of a professional identity. To be effective, these issues must be an integral part of the student's educational experience. To treat this critical area as an appendage to be tacked on during the waning days of social work education is to deprive the student, the profession, and potential users of services.

In addition to the contribution to curriculum development, the processes utilized by the project suggest a viable model for the necessary teamwork involving practitioners and educators. It reflects the long-standing commitment of the practice community to participation with educators in the education of competent practitioners.

THE BSW VIEW OF PRACTICE

Throughout the project, BSWs were involved in efforts to identify what entry level practitioners do and how well they feel they were prepared by their educational programs to do these activities, as well as to make suggestions for improving the ability of baccalaureate programs to prepare students for practice realities. This section summarizes the comments by BSWs involved at various points in project activities, drawing especially heavily upon contributions by participants at the BSW Practitioner Workshop held in New Orleans in 1976. The focus of these comments is on the realities that the entry level professional practitioner faces and the need for baccalaureate programs to insure that their graduates are ready to function effectively within these realities. It should be noted that the practitioners whose comments are summarized here graduated from baccalaureate programs one or more years before 1976 and that their reactions to their own educational experiences naturally reflect this fact.

Functioning in Organizations

BSW practitioners move into a variety of organizations and organizational positions. Many of them, especially in rural areas, are given responsibilities for program development, supervision, obtaining grants, and other administrative activities. In order to adapt to such wide-ranging activities, BSW practitioners felt that the entry level professional needs a range of intervention skills useable at the interpersonal as well as the organizational levels. This includes the ability to interpret professional social work roles in organizations that may be newly using social workers and the ability to develop support networks in the organization and/or the community in situations where the organization has few, if any, other social workers.

As baccalaureate social workers moved into organizations upon graduation, many felt unprepared for the stresses encountered within them. They felt that the entry level person must be able to analyze organizational objectives, structure, and levels of functioning so as to identify conflicts, opportunities, and formal and informal channels for everyday use. Since this often includes periods of frustration while trying to develop strategies to manage the sometimes cumbersome and conflicting aspects of organizations, practitioners must be prepared to cope and utilize support networks during these periods. BSWs noted that organizational functioning also requires some very basic work skills, such as writing letters, working with the media, budgeting, record keeping, planning of time, and the use of technical equipment. Finally, organizational functioning requires cooperative and collaborative activities with other professionals.

Practice Skills

As noted earlier, BSWs also indicated the need for a range of practice skills as basic for the functions they perform in the profession. Interviewing and assessment skills were considered essential, with assessment occurring in individual life situations as well as at community and organizational levels. Problem-solving and analysis skills were also clearly identified as important for the entry level practitioner, with analytical skills especially relevant for large institutional systems, the social welfare network, and community and organizational structures.

The telephone was noted as an important communication channel between practitioners and client populations, and entry level workers were said to need skill in being able to use the telephone as an intervention resource. Making connections between people, organizations, and other resources is an important part of the BSW's work and must include the ability to mobilize resources when necessary and appropriate. Indeed, the BSW practitioners felt that a significant part of their work was in linking people with resources, rather than doing in-depth counseling themselves.

Conceptions of change were seen to be sometimes unrealistic and not helpful. The practitioners saw a need for entry level professional social workers to see levels of change appropriate to organizational and community realities. For example, change objectives in private agencies may be quite different from those in public agencies, which often function within much more restrictive political mandates. Perceiving such levels of change helps BSWs to understand and work with resistance to change at both the individual and organizational levels. As resistance is encountered, the practitioners felt that entry level social workers need to be able to develop alternate strategies relevant to the change objectives.

Professional Identity

BSW practitioners felt that entry level professionals need to have a strong sense of professional identity and a broad view of the profession and how it affects service delivery. Since many work in organizations that offer few social work supports, the respondents believed that programs needed to ensure that their graduates had a strong sense of professional identity and established linkages with professional organizations. Indeed, many used faculty from the programs from which they graduated as an important part of their ongoing professional support system, and they felt this was an appropriate function for faculty to play. However, there was also some feeling that BSWs were not really accepted in professional organizations. They felt that these organizations needed to do much more to reach out to recruit BSWs and to integrate them into professional activities once they were members.

As a professional, the BSW practitioner needs to be able to assess his or her own functioning. The respondents felt that self-awareness in terms of personal values and professional functioning is extremely important, as is a strong commitment to correcting social injustices. Professional self-evaluation, in the view of these BSW practitioners, includes knowing when and where to seek help. In addition, many respondents expressed the need for baccalaureate programs to instill a developmental attitude in their students that supports the continuing search for and participation in educational and other professionally enriching growth activities.

Curriculum Content

The BSW practitioners had a number of comments about their own educational experiences and, based on their subsequent practice experiences, about ways in which curriculum content and program functioning could become more effective for the preparation of entry level professional practitioners. One was simply to improve the quality of instruction. A frequently mentioned correlate of this was the need to provide more and better connections between value and knowledge content and specific "how to" practice content. Many respondents felt that their education had been too theoretical and detached from practice realities, making it difficult for them to make the transition from the classroom to the field (in spite of field instruction in their academic programs).

Two content areas were identified as needing greater strength in order to prepare graduates for practice. One concerned the conditions that affect human behavior and that must be understood in the assessment, planning, and intervention processes. A second concerned the general area of research. Many respondents felt that further training was needed in such specific research-related techniques as data processing, computer programing, and statistics. This relates to the earlier cited need for BSWs to function in organizations in administrative capacities at various levels.

Finally, BSW practitioners indicated the need for baccalaureate programs to pay greater attention to the selection of students. Consistent with earlier expressed concerns about commitment, the tolerance of frustration, and the ability to function in a range of intervention situations, respondents looked to educational programs to screen out those persons not likely to function well in these areas.

NOTES

1. Pruger, Robert, "Bureaucratic Functioning as a Social Work Skill," in Appendix A.
2. Edward T. Weaver, Executive Director, American Public Welfare Association, personal communication.

 *Chapter 6*

Project Assumptions and Glossary

ASSUMPTIONS RELATED TO PRACTICE AND THE PROFESSION

1. The entry level of professional practice in social work requires the content areas as specified by CSWE accreditation standards for baccalaureate programs. This is consistent with the official policy of the National Association of Social Workers.

2. The following definition of social work is utilized by the project[1] : Social work is concerned and involved with the interactions between people and the institutions of society that affect the ability of people to accomplish life tasks, realize aspirations and values, and alleviate distress. These interactions between people and the social institutions in which people function occur within the context of the larger societal good. Therefore, three major purposes of social work may be identified: (a) to enhance the problem-solving, coping, and developmental capacities of people; (b) to promote the effective and humane operation of the systems that provide people with resources and services;[2] and (c) to link people with systems that provide them with resources, services, and opportunities.[3]

3. Social work has a historic commitment to the oppressed and less advantaged; this commitment, which needs to be renewed and revitalized periodically, continues to be a priority of the profession. This project accepts responsibility for helping with this task and therefore assumes that all social workers *must* have, as essential to the basics for entry level practice, the knowledge, values, and skills necessary to operationalize this commitment. This is not to be

viewed as counter or contradictory to the profession's ongoing concern for the enhancement of the quality of life for all people.

4. Social change toward the goals of improving social conditions and social functioning for all persons is an integral part of social work practice. It is the responsibility of every social worker to attempt to contribute to the achievement of these goals.

5. Every social work practitioner has the responsibility to understand the interrelationship between "private troubles" and "public issues," since they are but two aspects of a problem. Every social worker should have sufficient knowledge and skill to assess when to intervene or not to intervene at various system levels so as to effect feasible goal achievement, recognizing the limits of one's competence and the need to call upon necessary resources.

6. Many BSWs will be in settings where professional support systems are weak or even nonexistent. In such settings, the BSW will need to develop professional support systems as feasible and, when necessary, to clarify and interpret the role and contribution of professional social work.

7. BSWs will work within an organizational context, most freqently within the complex organization, both governmental and nongovernmental.

8. Continued competence in practice requires that there be available to the practitioner a range of learning opportunities that build upon the basic undergraduate curriculum content (e.g., staff developlment, continuing education, supervision, consultation, and advanced education). The BSW must be prepared to utilize these opportunities for continued professional development.

ASSUMPTIONS RELATED TO SOCIAL WORK EDUCATION

1. The primary aim of baccalaureate social work education is to prepare an entry level professional *practitioner*. As such, the definition of knowledge, values, and skills content required at the baccalaureate level must reflect the demands of practice at the entry level insofar as it is possible to do so given the great variance in utilization of the BSW practitioner at the present time.

2. There is basic curriculum content that can be identified and that should be mastered by all graduates of accredited baccalaureate programs prior to entering professional practice in social work. Presently, this basic content is loosely defined in the CSWE accredi-

tation standards. It is assumed that the basic content can be identified and defined with greater precision and clarity; such was the assumption upon which this project was funded by the Social and Rehabilitation Service of HEW.

3. The fundamentals, or basics, for entry level professional practice in social work includes the professional core as well as content relevant for practice from supporting disciplines. *The professional core*, as it is defined by the project, includes the knowledge, values, and skills that in constellation are unique and specific to the social work profession and to the practice of social work. Knowledge and skill content drawn from supporting disciplines is also part of preparation for entry level practice in social work, but such content may also be shared with other professions (e.g., interviewing and other communication skills).

4. The material developed by the project identifies the fundamental content that should be included in any accredited baccalaureate social work educational program. It is assumed that each school will develop its own curriculum model for the teaching of the content, with the particular model selected reflecting any instituion's specific needs, objectives, and resources.

5. The project aims to identify only that fundamental content (knowledge, values, and skills) that must be mastered if the graduate is to be competent to practice as an entry level professional social worker. It is assumed that most educational programs would exceed and go beyond the minimal content, including preparation for practice in more specialized areas such as in special settings, fields of practice, or with particular population groups.

6. Mastery of the content that is basic and minimal to the achievement of the fundamental "practice competencies" is not accomplished in social work courses alone. Rather, the minimal content includes essential liberal education components, including basic foundation content from other academic disciplines in the college or university. Achievement of the fundamental content will normally encompass the four academic years; however, clarity of objectives and fundamental content should make it possible for programs to adapt to students' prior educational and life experiences.

7. Mastery of the fundamental content is the first step in preparation for a career in social work. It is assumed, therefore, that the basics are applicable to any practice setting, as contrasted to preparation for a specific setting, and that the basics will be built upon and enriched in a variety of ways throughout the individual's professional career.

NOTES

1. Initially, the project utilized the NASW working definition of social work and social work practice, which reads as follows: "Social Work is the professional activity of helping individuals, groups, or communities enhance or restore their capacity for social functioning and creating societal conditions favorable to this goal. Social work practice consists of the professional application of social work values, principles, and techniques to one or more of the following ends: helping people obtain tangible services; counseling or psychotherapy with individuals, families, and groups; helping communities or groups provide or improve social and health services; and participating in relevant legislative processes." (National Association of Social Workers, "Standards of Social Services Manpower," Washington, D.C., 1974, pp. 4-5). For a variety of reasons, this definition was not acceptable to those involved with the Curriculum Development Project. It was anticipated that NASW would provide a clearer definition; when it was unable to do so, project staff adapted a definition originally presented by Allen Pincus and Anne Minahan in *Social Work Practice: Model and Method* (Itasca, Illinois: Peacock, 1973).

2. People now and always will need systems for resources and services. "Promote," as it is used here, includes increasing the responsiveness of already existing systems, as well as stimulating new arrangements and even terminating those that may no longer be helpful or that affect people adversely.

3. See Chapter 7, Part I, for additional detail on the project's definition of social work.

GLOSSARY

This glossary is provided to clarify for the reader the way in which key terms are used by this project. Many of these terms have been used in several different ways in the professional social work literature, and it is hoped that this glossary will help the reader to avoid confusion by clarifying exactly which meaning is intended in this document.

Activity—A specific action or sphere of action.
Basic (fundamental) content—The professional core, plus knowledge and skill content drawn from supporting disciplines that may also be shared with other professions.
Client population—Individuals, groups, or organizations that are the recipients of the benefits of the professional peoples use of themselves in professional ways.
Competency (competence)—Possession of sufficient required skill, knowledge, qualification, or capacity for a stated purpose.
Diverse groups—The notion of diverse groups has to be understood in

a complex and developmental context that can include both as-cribed and self-designated categories that are neither mutually exclusive (e.g., age and ethnicity) nor necessarily interchangeable (e.g., ethnic-cultural groups). Diversity is to be understood as on a continuum.

Entry level practitioners—The practitioner who has attained the basic fundamental competencies for professional practice in social work, as these are defined by CSWE and NASW.

Function—Appropriate activities to carry out designated objectives.

Objective—The aim, or intended end, of action.

Professional core—The knowledge, values, and skills that in constella-tion are unique and specific to the social work profession and to the practice of social work.

Purpose—The reason for which something is done.

Skill—The ability to perform actions based on knowledge, experi-ence, and aptitude.

System—The elements or items forming a complex or unitary whole.

Teach—To impart knowledge or skill in situations, building on exist-ing knowledge and skill, and involving the person(s) being taught in a reciprocal exchange of ideas, information, and skills.

Chapter 7

Objectives, Functions, and Activities for Entry Level Professional Practice in Social Work

This project's major goal was to identify basic objectives and curriculum content for the preparation of entry level professional social workers. In order to achieve this goal, the project had to develop a clearer picture of what the entry level practitioner should be prepared to do in practice. This chapter presents the results of the process, fully described in Chapter 4, used to define the objectives, the functions, and the activities appropriate and essential for the entry level practitioner toward the achievement of the overall purposes of the profession of social work.

For purposes of clarity, this chapter is divided into three parts. Part I presents the project's definition of social work and its purposes. Part II details the objectives, functions, and illustrative entry level professional activities that comprise the social work problem-solving process. These objectives, functions, and illustrative activities are not ends in themselves. Rather, they are seen by this project as tools that are essential for the attainment of the purposes of social work. Part III of this chapter describes the objectives, functions, and illustrative entry level professional activities that are specifically related to the achievement of the purposes of social work. The performance of these activities assumes mastery of all of the elements described in Part II, the problem-solving process.

Throughout this chapter, a focus on the values and ethics, as well as the purposes, of the profession is essential. The activities listed become social work practice activities only when they are performed within the ethical framework of the profession. Without the ethical foundation, or without being related to purpose, they become simply techniques that lack professional meaning and sanction.

Finally, the activities listed are identified as "illustrative." Obviously, many different activities can be, and are, utilized to achieve a common objective. Indeed, as techniques improve, activities may change dramatically. It is important, therefore, to recognize the activities identified as "illustrative" only.

PART I—THE PURPOSES OF SOCIAL WORK

Social work is concerned and involved with the interactions between people and the institutions of society[1] that affect the ability of people to accomplish life tasks, realize aspirations and values, and alleviate distress. These interactions between people and social institutions occur within the context of the larger societal good. Therefore, three major purposes of social work may be identified:

1. to enhance the problem-solving, coping, and developmental capacities of people;
2. to promote the effective and humane operation of the systems that provide people with resources and services;
3. to link people with systems that provide them with resources,[2] services, and opportunities.[3]

These purposes direct the practice of all social workers, including those at the entry level of practice. They do so through a series of objectives and functions that make it possible to achieve the three purposes and through specific activities that operationalize the functions. Activities become significant professional practice activities only when they are explictly related to the purposes and functions of social work. Given the objectives of this project, the activities identified below will be those essential for all practitioners at the entry level of professional social work practice.

NOTES

1. This project defines the institutions of society as including the family, education, religion, political and economic institutions, and the social welfare institution (including the health, legal, criminal justice, financial assistance, and social services systems and structures). The interactions between people and the institutions of society may include interactions between people within one institution (family members, for example), the functioning of one person in attempting to carry out institutional roles (an aged widow, for example), people attempting to interact with structures (a family seeking public assistance, for

example), or institutional structures in interactions that influence people's lives (a social work agency's participation in the political process, for example).

2. The project utilizes the conception of "resource" developed by Max Siporin, i.e., "any valuable thing, on reserve or at hand, that one can mobilize and put to instructional use in order to function, meet a need or resolve a problem" (Max Siporin, *Introduction to Social Work Practice* [New York: MacMillan, 1975], p. 22). Resource in this context includes the worker as a resource, social services, rights and benefits, entitlements, client resources, etc.

3. This definition is adopted from Allen Pincus and Anne Minahan, *Social Work Practice: Model and Method* (Itasca, Illinois: Peacock, 1973). It is also similar to the definition of social work developed by Werner W. Boehm in the earlier CSWE curriculum study. See Werner W. Boehm, "Statement on the Nature of Social Work," in *Objectives for the Social Work Curriculum of the Future* (New York: Council on Social Work Education, 1959).

PART II—THE OBJECTIVES, FUNCTIONS, AND ACTIVITIES RELATED TO THE PROBLEM-SOLVING PROCESS

Overall Purpose

The purpose of social work problem solving is to gain skill in the processes of problem solving within the values and ethics of the profession of social work and is directed toward the achievement of the purposes of social work. This purpose underlies the four objectives of the problem-solving process.

Objective 1. To identify and assess situations where the relationship between people and social institutions needs to be initiated, enhanced, restored, protected, or terminated.

Function 1. To collect necessary information for the purpose of problem or situation identification and assessment.

Illustrative Entry Level Activities.

1. Assesses willingness, or options, of the client population to participate in the assessment process.
2. Involves client population in information-gathering process to the most relevant extent possible, explaining and interpreting the purposes, content, and questions.
3. Identifies, makes contact with, and obtains information from others (lay and professional) whose involvement is critical to the data collection and assessment processes.
4. Collects, reviews, and evaluates written or verbal information received from service system colleagues or citizens.
5. Interviews client population, securing social history and background information (as pertinent), presenting situation information, and other pertinent data.
6. Observes client population to note any obvious discrepancies in self-reported information such as physical well-being, behaviors, group interactions, etc.
7. Clarifies values of client population, identifying areas of similarity and difference between client, worker, and agency.
8. Identifies, studies, and analyzes relevant institutional policies and procedures that directly affect and relate to specific client situation, requesting clarification when necessary.
9. Utilizes prior studies and surveys relevant literature and/or other sources for data and ideas relevant to an understanding of the situation about which assessment is needed.

10. Summarizes and analyzes that data which is pertinent for the clear formulation of an assessment.

Objective 1.

Function 2. To make special efforts to identify services and resources needed by those populations most vulnerable or discriminated against.

Illustrative Entry Level Activities.

1. Collects data and identifies population groups within the community most at risk.
2. Collects data and identifies service-resource allocation gaps to at risk population group members within worker's own case-service assignment.
3. Identifies real and potential obstacles to groups that are especially vulnerable or discriminated against, securing services and/or resources for those within the worker's own service unit.
4. Surveys relevant literature to develop ideas and plan for ways in which the types of obstacles to service that groups that are especially vulnerable or discriminated against encounter can be minimized and/or overcome.

Objective 1.

Function 3. To utilize the data collected to make an assessment of the problem or situation with and/or for the client population.

Illustrative Entry Level Activities.

1. Uses mutual assessment to reach a preliminary problem or situation definition by articulating problems and concerns.
2. Determines with client population appropriateness of agency and its resources for the service needed and/or desired.
3. When indicated by the preliminary problem assessment, refers to more appropriate resources and assists in making contacts and linkages.

Objective 2. To develop and implement a plan for improving the well-being of the client population based on the problem or situation assessment and exploration of obtainable goals and available options.

Function 1. To arrive at mutual agreement with the client population on an interventive plan.

Illustrative Entry Level Activities.

1. Collects necessary information for the development of an interventive plan, utilizing available data, relevant literature, past experience, and the expertness of others (including supervisors, peers, other colleagues, community citizens, and others).
2. Shares with the client population available information relevant to the development of an intervention plan.
3. Discusses situation with client population, formulating realistic interventive objectives and goals, identifying options and alternatives, and indicating relevant resources that are available and potential.
4. Develops an intervention-action plan with the client population, taking into account client choices, resources, feasibility, organizational policies, and possibilities as well as constraints.

Objective 2.

Function 2. To utilize the unique strengths, abilities, and skills of people of diverse backgrounds in the development and implementation of plans to accomplish the desired objectives.

Illustrative Entry Level Activities.

1. Confers with and learns from client population in order to continually enhance the worker's own understanding of cultural, ethnic, racial, sexual, and lifestyle uniqueness and difference.
2. Identifies and analyzes the style, culture, strengths, and capabilities of client populations with diverse backgrounds and characteristics.
3. Assists client population in articulating ways in which services and resources can become more responsive to particular client groups.

Objective 2.

Function 3. To reasses the situation periodically and modify interventive plan(s) as indicated.

Illustrative Entry Level Activities.

1. Engages the client population in ongoing evaluation of the understanding of the problem and the effectiveness of the action plan.
2. Analyzes new relevant information that becomes available or new conditions that alter the problem or situation.
3. Modifies the interventive plan with the assistance of the client as indicated.

Objective 3. To evaluate the extent to which the objectives of the worker's intervention were achieved.

Function 1. To develop criteria for use in evaluating the intervention plan.

Illustrative Entry Level Activities.

1. Reviews and critically evaluates research findings and personal practice experiences pertinent to the situation at hand.
2. Identifies assessment criteria that are relevant to the intervention objectives.
3. Contracts with the client population, agreeing on the goal attainment activities appropriate for those involved in intervention activities and the times and methods of assessment of intervention activities.

Objective 3.

Function 2. To collect and use data pertinent to the evaluation of the intervention plan.

Illustrative Entry Level Activities.

1. Assists with the development and use of various methods for securing direct client feedback on services and/or resources received.
2. Records observations and information pertinent to the progress of the intervention plan.
3. Uses the data collected to evaluate the intervention outcomes and to plan for future activities and intervention strategies.

Objective 4. To support and uphold the standards and ethics of the profession toward the improvement of services and resources for people.

Function 1. To participate with colleagues in activities that foster professional growth and development.

Illustrative Entry Level Activities.

1. Holds membership in and participates in activities of professional association(s).
2. Develops a support system by identifying peers and others with whom one relates in a professionally productive way.
3. Consults with colleagues regarding knowledge, techniques, or skills, exchanging information as appropriate.
4. Participates with colleagues in identifying continuing education needs and in planning for meeting these needs.
5. Attends and participates in training sessions, workshops, institutes, and seminars.
6. Participates with colleagues in informal and formal activities sponsored by professional association(s).
7. Makes available one's own practice observations and data to appropriate persons or groups for their use in improving the profession's knowledge and skill base.

Objective 4.

Function 2. To evaluate and improve one's own professional functioning and effectiveness.

Illustrative Entry Level Activities.

1. Utilizes data collected from one's own service delivery activities to modify, adapt, and/or improve one's own practice.
2. Studies the profession's literature, keeping current with research studies related to interventions and their effectiveness, as well as other pertinent policy and practice issues.
3. Develops tools and/or utilizes agency procedures for carrying out periodic self-evaluation of one's own professional functioning.
4. Identifies and consults with colleagues, including those from other professions, to gain additional knowledge and insight related to specific situations.
5. Requests "feedback" on professional functioning from colleagues, client-consumer(s), and others as appropriate.

Objective 4.

Function 3. To participate with professional colleagues in the professional association directed toward the development, implementation, and maintenance of standards for professional practice and service delivery.

Illustrative Entry Level Activities.

1. Keeps current on the activities of the professional association in the area of standards and ethics by utilizing professional news sources.
2. Participates or otherwise supports activities promoted by the profession designed to stimulate, promote, and maintain the ethics of the profession.
3. Provides input through available channels to assist in the development of standards by the professional association.
4. Assists in the improvement of service delivery through efforts to bring about greater conformity of agencies to established professional standards.
5. Works for the public awareness and adoption of recognized standards for social work practice through public education and appropriate legislative efforts.

PART III—THE OBJECTIVES, FUNCTIONS, AND ACTIVITIES RELATED TO THE PURPOSES OF SOCIAL WORK

Overall Objective

The objective in carrying out the purposes of social work is to enhance the interactions between people and the institutions of society that affect their lives.

Purpose 1. To enhance the problem-solving, coping, and developmental capacities of people.

Function 1. To teach the client population skills in attaining and utilizing resources throughout the helping process.

Illustrative Entry Level Activities.

1. Assists the client population with the development of skills to analyze one's own and others' needs, including skills to determine if the acquisition, modification, or improvement of services and/or resources is needed.
2. Teaches the client population knowledge about community resources (what they are and how to secure and utilize them), including consumer rights and legal procedures.
3. Assists the client population with the examination of action alternatives and the consideration of possible consequences of actions taken.
4. Teaches the client population leadership and participation skills in the use of groups for individual, group, and community development and action.
5. Assists the client population with the development of skills needed to implement action plans, including skills for drawing upon professional and other resources for technical assistance.

Purpose 1.

Function 2. To assist the client population with the development of groups of common social and community concern and/or to make linkage with such groups.

Illustrative Entry Level Activities.

1. Assists the client population to identify issues of common social and community concern.
2. Assists the client population to identify the resource networks available and to make contact and linkage with them.
3. Assists the client population to develop and/or form new resource systems as may be appropriate.
4. Provides information and/or consultation to self-help resources in areas within the worker's competence.

Overall Objective

The objective in carrying out the purposes of social work is to en-hance the interactions between people and the institutions of society which affect their lives.

Purpose 2. To link people with systems that provide them with resources, services, and opportunities.

Function 1. To establish linkages between people and resource systems.

Illustrative Entry Level Activities.

1. Participates in identifying and locating people in need of or eligible for particular resources or benefits.
2. Provides information to the client population regarding avail-able resources, agency regulations and sanctions, what services and resources they are entitled to, and procedures to follow in applying for services.
3. Assists the client population with the development of knowl-edge and skills necessary to interpret needs and concerns to resource system(s).
4. Makes referral(s) to needed resource(s) and assists the client population with getting the resource(s) needed.
5. Assists the client population with overcoming obstacles that may discourage or prevent securing and/or utilizing needed resources.
6. Uses data from one's own case-service load to inform one's supervisor-administrators of problems that a resource system's procedures may have for present and potential client popula-tions.
7. Collects and transmits helpful and appropriate information about clients to resource systems, within legal limits and pro-fessional ethics.
8. Interprets special needs and/or rights of groups that are es-pecially vulnerable or discriminated against to peers, colleagues, and relevant others in the resource system.
9. Interprets and/or advocates on behalf of clients to relevant resources, using such strategies as are appropriate.
10. Assists colleagues with the development of coordinated service plans when requested, to provide the clients with needed resources.

11. Mediates between client(s) and the resource system, as may be appropriate and necessary for the client population to secure needed resources.

Purpose 2.

Function 2. To facilitate interaction and to modify and build relationships between people within the resource system (including client populations).

Illustrative Entry Level Activities.

1. Identifies and clarifies behaviors and actions within the client population that are dysfunctional to the well-being of the total client system.
2. Assists with interpreting problems, concerns, and/or issues within the client population to other individuals and groups within the system.
3. Identifies and clarifies changes and modifications in behaviors and actions necessary for the client to function more harmoniously.
4. Mediates within parts of the client system as may be necessary.
5. Assists (teaches) the client population in the development of coping and/or adaptive behaviors when they are an appropriate part of the mutually negotiated intervention plan
6. Identifies and mobilizes internal and external resources needed and useful to the client population in modifying, building, and changing relationships.
7. Interprets-advocates for the rights of all members of the client system.

Purpose 2.

Function 3. To use the authority granted by agencies legally mandated to impose courses of action on the client population to facilitate and restore interaction between people and societal resource systems.

Illustrative Entry Level Activities.

1. Interprets to the client population social work purposes and roles within the legal authority granted to the agency and carried out by the social worker.
2. Assists the client population with understanding the consequences of violating a legally prescribed course of action.
3. Interprets the client population's special needs, problems, and situation to the appropriate part of the resource system.
4. Identifies-reviews client population and/or agency failure to carry out agreed upon service plans.
5. Negotiates and/or renegotiates a service plan most helpful and feasible for the client population.
6. Assists the client population with the development of skills and/or modifications-adaptations of behaviors as may be necessary to cope with the client population environment.
7. Advocates for the client population as may be necessary, utilizing strategies appropriate to the situation.

Overall Objective

The objective in carrying out the purposes of social work is to enhance the interactions between people and institutions of society which affect their lives.

Purpose 3. To promote the effective and humane operation of the systems that provide people with resources and services.

Function 1. To perform agency procedures creatively, accurately, and with maximum effectiveness for facilitating service delivery activities.

Illustrative Entry Level Activities.

1. Studies and analyzes the objectives, programs, procedures, regulations, practices, and policies of an agency or organization.
2. Explains and interprets agency or organization program, policies, and procedures to policy groups, other agency personnel, client populations, and others as appropriate.
3. Develops one's own personal work plan, with objectives and priorities identified.
4. Reviews case files or client records, becoming familiar with the case situation.
5. Develops and presents service plans to colleagues and/or supervisor.
6. Prepares periodic summaries of case-service activity for presentation to staff, referral agencies, and others as appropriate.
7. Authorizes services, using one's personal authority within established procedures.
8. Records case-service activities according to established procedures.
9. Drafts regular and special memos, letters, oral presentations, minutes, and/or reports when needed for agency reporting and decisionmaking, and compiles information as needed, using established agency or organization procedures.
10. Confers-consults with service system colleagues, including supervisors, regarding work plans, case-service situations, and administrative policies and procedures.
11. Attends and participates in staff meetings, discussing and articulating issues and concerns, clarifying points, and exchanging information as appropriate.

Purpose 3.

Function 2.   To work with others within one's agency or organization in efforts to improve service quality within the agency or organization.

Illustrative Entry Level Activities.

1. Collects data on responsiveness, appropriateness, or omission of client services or resources in relation to need that emerges from one's own case-service load.
2. Identifies appropriate individuals or groups within the agency or organization for presentation of data that has been collected and analyzed.
3. Describes unmet service or resource needs to appropriate service supervisors, peers, agency or organization staff members, and others, using relevant data as appropriate.
4. Develops a "support network" of peers, colleagues, and others within the existing framework of the agency or organization.
5. Participates in developing plans with peers, supervisors, and/or colleagues for eliminating, modifying, or adapting an agency practice or policy that could improve agency responses to client populations and that is within the purview of the worker's practice area.
6. Participates in planning details of new service programs with service system colleagues and the client population affected.
7. Assists with the implementation of new service plans, or whatever portions are feasible, within the existing agency framework, making use of a support network of others.

Purpose 3.

Function 3.   To identify resource gaps, service inequities, and dysfunctional social conditions to colleagues, the profession(s), and other private groups.

Illustrative Entry Level Activities.

1. Collects and summarizes data from one's own caseload regarding service inequities, utilizing colleagues for assistance as appropriate.
2. Consults with colleagues, supervisors, and/or others on the development of a plan or strategy to most effectively present data to appropriate groups.

3. Presents data to administrators, supervisors, colleagues, citizen groups, and/or professional association(s) as appropriate.

Purpose 3.

Function 4. To participate with colleagues and others in activities toward the improvement of community conditions, services, and resources.

Illustrative Entry Level Activities.

1. Participates in community planning groups and other organizations concerned with community planning, change, and improvement.
2. Studies the local, state, and federal legislative processes involved in the creation and passage of legislation.
3. Assists with the development of a position paper that outlines a community group's or the professional association(s) stance on current policy issues.
4. Consults with citizen organizations and members of professional association(s) on specific areas within the worker's professional competence.
5. Contributes ideas for new service programs with members of professional association(s), community planning groups, or other relevant organizations within the community.
6. Participates in community activities and programs that are actively concerned and involved with decreasing discrimination and injustice.

Purpose 3.

Function 5. To utilize the organization as a resource to affect community conditions that adversely affect people.

Illustrative Entry Level Activities.

1. To identify the range and variety of actual and potential resources within the agency or organization and/or to which the agency or organization has access.
2. To identify ways in which the range of resources within the agency can be brought to bear on one's own case-service load.
3. To interpret the resources of the agency or organization to citizen-client population groups and to public and private societal resource systems.
4. To identify and articulate to supervisors, administrators, and/or colleagues ways in which the resources of the agency are germane to specific community problems or situations.

Chapter 8

Competencies of the Entry Level
Professional Social Worker

The ten basic competencies deemed essential to the entry level educational program are identified in this chapter.

They were developed from the content of the preceding chapter, which detailed the purposes, objectives, functions, and illustrative entry level professional practice activities. Presumably, these competencies all together constitute the basics, or fundamentals, for entry level professional practice in social work.

In presenting the basic competencies, some observations are in order. First, the competencies are broadly stated. This was done consciously and deliberately because project staff believe that in the process of moving toward the establishment of a basic curriculum in social work education, it is important that flexibility be retained. Such, it would seem, is important for professional education, which must always be responsive to changes in its cultural and societal environment. Thus, the competencies, which hopefully will serve as the cornerstone for strengthening the basic curriculum, will also equally hopefully provide curriculum developers with direction, but without constriction and rigidity. Of course, faculty in their own programs may choose to define anticipated outcomes more specifically. Such would be entirely appropriate as the project material is utilized to stimulate faculty creativity and ingenuity. Second, these competencies encompass the minimum which should be included in the basic curriculum. They do not, in this sense, represent the totality of any individual curricula. This project assumes that each program will have a unique set of objectives. All programs will include as preparation for entry level professional practice the basic competencies that are described in this project, as well as other objectives or competencies that are both consistent with entry level practice and relevant to the unique mission and environment of a particular program. Third, the competencies as stated do not indicate degree or level of competence. The intention of the competency in terms of level is, in this document, best expressed through the activities described in the preceding chapter. This project has not developed tools for the assessment of competency. That is clearly a task for the future, and one which is even now being addressed by individual educational programs as well as by the National Association of Social Workers.

In the presentation of the competencies that follows, each competency is stated and then followed by a paragraph that describes illustrative specific competencies necessary to achieve the more general competency. These illustrations are provided in order to suggest the scope of activities that comprise the general competency. They also serve to help identify specific competencies that are part of more than one general competency. Finally, the order in which the competencies are presented does not infer any ranking in terms of sequence or importance. It simply attempts to provide a logical ordering of competencies, each of which is an equally important part of the entry level professional practitioner's identity.

THE TEN COMPETENCIES

1. *Identify and assess situations where the relationship between people and social institutions needs to be initiated, enhanced, restored, protected, or terminated.*

Includes use of methods of data collection and analysis, including electronic technology for these purposes; interviewing, observation and recording; review and analysis of institutional policies and procedures; involvement of the client population in the data collection and assessment processes to the fullest extent possible; carrying out data collection and assessment processes with involuntary clients; collaboration and teamwork with others relevant to the data collection and assessment processes; use of interpersonal skills and relationships with individuals and groups.

2. *Develop and implement a plan for improving the well-being of people based on problem assessment and the exploration of obtainable goals and available options.*

Includes involvement of client populations in the planning and implementation processes to the fullest extent possible; planning for and working with involuntary clients humanely and sensitively; planning and implementing plans within the ethics of social work;

learning about and utilizing the distinctive strengths of each individual and each cultural and lifestyle group; collaboration and teamwork with relevant others or groups outside the client system in planning and implementing plans.

3. Enhance the problem-solving, coping, and developmental capacities of people.

Includes provision of information; provision of support; teaching people useful skills; facilitating interaction between people with mutual interests or concerns individually and through the use of groups; use of indigenous helping networks and resources; respect for and use of unique strengths and resources of diverse individuals and groups; helping the involuntary client with support when necessary and with the exploration of more rewarding behaviors when possible; use of the problem-solving model; helping client populations make use of (or better use of) existing services, resources, opportunities; making use of interpersonal skills and relationships with individuals and groups, being aware of one's own values about people and groups.

4. Link people with systems that provide them with resources, services, and opportunities.

Includes knowledge of relevant systems; use of the self-help and indigenous helping networks; initiating self-help activities when appropriate; obtaining and disseminating information, making use of electronic technology as available; clarifying procedures and objectives; mediating between people and systems; facilitating communication and interaction; providing support to people needing or seeking resources, services, opportunities; monitoring structures to insure their humane, equitable, and helpful treatment of people; referring people to the most appropriate service-resource opportunity.

5. Intervene effectively on behalf of populations most vulnerable and discriminated against.

Includes collection and analysis of caseload and printed data about such populations; outreach efforts to identify and reach these populations; sensitivity to priorities, need definitions, and resources used by diverse groups; facilitating changes in policies and legislation that impede the provision of resources or services to vulnerable populations; advocating for needed services; assisting in the development of needed resources and services; use of existing services and resources and of protective legislation to supplement and support indigenous resources; use of professional standards and ethics when evaluating services, resources, opportunities provided to people; being aware of one's own values regarding human diversity; educating resource systems about the needs of vulnerable populations through the provision of relevant information.

6. Promote the effective and humane operation of the systems that provide people with services, resources, and opportunities.

Includes the maximum use of agency policies and structures to facilitate the provision of services, resources, opportunities to people; analysis of agency planning and policymaking structures; participation in activities to improve and/or initiate agency services and procedures; development of a collegial support network; use of interpersonal skills and relationships with individuals and groups; timely and efficient performance of agency procedures; participation in agency decisionmaking as appropriate; use of professional standards and ethics as a guide when functioning in agencies and other helping systems; special sensitivity to the needs of involuntary clients; collection and analysis of caseload and printed data, and making it available to appropriate persons in helping systems.

7. Actively participate with others in creating new, modified, or improved service, resource, opportunity systems that are more equitable, just, and responsive to consumers of services, and work with others to eliminate those systems that are unjust.

Includes methods of evaluative research; planning; policymaking; involvement of client populations in planning and policymaking as much as possible; creation of support networks in resource and helping systems; sensitivity to the needs of involuntary clients who may not be able to express them or affect service delivery; use of professional standards and ethics; use of personal power and influence; work with colleagues to initiate and/or support changes in dysfunctional agency policies and practices.

8. Evaulate the extent to which the objectives of the intervention plan were achieved.

Includes the formulation and utilization of devices to measure intervention success or failure; use of methods of data collection and analysis, including electronic technology for these purposes; involving client populations in the evaluation process; use of evaluative data to renegotiate the service plan as appropriate; consulting with colleagues about intervention strategies.

9. Continually evaluate one's own professional growth and development through assessment of practice behaviors and skills.

Includes use of methods of data collection and analysis about one's own practice activities and their effects; obtaining feedback from client populations; obtaining feedback from colleagues; using professional standards and ethics as a framework to evaluate one's own practice; reading and drawing upon current scientific and practice literature; ongoing participation in continuing education; increasing self-awareness.

10. Contribute to the improvement of service delivery by adding to the knowledge base of the profession as appropriate and by supporting and upholding the standards and ethics of the profession.

Includes personal involvement in the activities of professional associations; thorough knowledge of professional standards and ethics; ongoing involvement in professional continuing education programs; collaboration with colleagues in activities to advocate for or support professional standards and ethics in legislation and places of employment; ongoing assessment of one's own practice; using one's own practice experience as a basis for contributing to the knowledge base of the profession.

Chapter 9

Knowledge, Values, and Skills Essential for the Attainment of the Entry Level Competencies: A Summary

Having identified the entry level professional social work competencies, it is possible to develop the basic curriculum content that will enable baccalaureate level students to attain these competencies. The project has divided this content into two parts: basic skills and basic knowledge. Both the skills and the knowledge have been derived directly from each competency, and in Appendix B each competency is listed with the skills and knowledge essential for its attainment. This appendix also details the subsections for each skill and knowledge category.

This chapter presents the skill and knowledge content in summary form and is divided into two parts. The first is a summary listing of the basic skills content necessary for a baccalaureate curriculum to prepare competent entry level professional social work practitioners. In order to facilitate clarity of presentation, the skills are organized under four headings: information gathering and assessment; the development and use of the professional self; practice activities with individuals, groups, and communities, as well as within organizations; and evaluation of professional activities. These headings and the order of skills under each are simply for clarity of presentation. They do not in any way infer a preferred sequential order or a ranking in terms of importance. Full details of the component parts of each skill may be found in Appendix B.

The second part of the chapter is a summary listing of the fundamental knowledge content necessary for a baccalaureate curriculum to prepare competent entry level professional social work practitioners. In order to facilitate clarity of presentation, the knowledge items are organized under five headings: the cultural context of social welfare and social work; human functioning at the individual, group, and community levels; the social foundations of human need; the structure of societal responses to meet human need; and strategies for professional intervention to achieve planned change. As with the skill content in part one, these headings and the order of knowledge categories under each are simply for clarity of presentation. No ranking in terms of importance or sequence is inferred. Full details of the component parts of each knowledge category may be found in Appendix B.

It may seem strange that there is no separate listing of fundamental value content for a baccalaureate curriculum preparing competent entry level professional social work practitioners. Obviously this project believes that such value content is crucial. However, it also believes that the value dimensions of the profession and professional practice can best be included as knowledge and skill components in the curriculum. Content about values can be taught as knowledge about values themselves, a society's multiplicity of values, the uses of values, etc. It can also be taught in terms of skills, ways in which values get translated into ethical practice behaviors. This project's definition of social work, including its purposes, objectives, and functions, states that values and ethics give professional sanction and significance to practice activities. This point of view is carried forward into the curriculum content by integrating values and ethics into the knowledge and skills that are basic to the preparation of the entry level professional social work practitioner.

Finally, we need to point out that while every effort was made to include the critical knowledge, value, and skill components, there is no intent to imply that *all* of the necessary content is identified. The state of the art does not permit such a presumption at this time. We also believe that if there is greater clarity regarding the intended educational outcomes—i.e., the competencies—there is less need to define the knowledge, value, and skill components narrowly.

PART ONE—FUNDAMENTAL SKILLS

I. Information Gathering and Assessment
   A. Developing awareness of others
      1. Understanding human diversity
      2. Responding to human diversity
   B. Obtaining information
      1. Observing activities and situations
      2. Obtaining feedback

      3. Carrying out research activities
        a. Selecting an appropriate research strategy
        b. Developing research variables
        c. Collecting data
        d. Analyzing data
   C. Evaluating resources
   D. Interpreting and assessing
   E. Analyzing policy
   F. Identifying social problems

II. The Development and Use of the Professional Self
   A. Maintaining professional identity
      1. Joining professional organizations
      2. Organizing professional activities
      3. Supporting professional ethics
      4. Using professional ethics
      5. Clarifying professional standards
      6. Respecting others
      7. Relating to others
   B. Interpreting professional roles
   C. Writing effectively for professional communication
   D. Managing professional resources
      1. Collaborating with professional colleagues
      2. Using consultation appropriately
      3. Utilizing one's own professional self
   E. Continuing professional growth

III. Practice Activities with Individuals, Groups, and Communities, as Well as Within Organizations
   A. Managing data and information
      1. Using communication channels
      2. Communicating effectively
      3. Promoting communication
      4. Interviewing
      5. Hearing
      6. Translating communications
      7. Providing information
      8. Providing feedback
      9. Summarizing content
      10. Interpreting and using data
      11. Presenting data
      12. Presenting plans
   B. Managing relationships

      1. Developing understanding
      2. Interacting with others
      3. Facilitating interaction
      4. Facilitating interpersonal activities
      5. Clarifying attitudes and feelings
      6. Clarifying implications of choices
      7. Working collaboratively with others
      8. Involving others
      9. Supporting and encouraging
    10. Helping others develop positive self-images
    11. Motivating others
    12. Teaching others

C. Managing situations
      1. Using human diversity as a component of practice
      2. Involving client populations in practice activities
      3. Involving community persons in practice activities
      4. Facility in problem solving
         a. Identifying goals
         b. Identifying types of plans
         c. Selecting appropriate intervention strategies
      5. Monitoring service delivery
      6. Using systems
         a. Using indigenous helping networks
         b. Using family, group, community networks
         c. Developing community support networks
         d. Supporting activities of citizen groups
      7. Contracting
         a. Renegotiating contracts
      8. Mediating
      9. Mobilizing
    10. Advocating
    11. Using personal power
    12. Using conflict and confrontation
    13. Referring persons

D. Managing organizational activities
      1. Functioning effectively in organizations
         a. Facilitating organizational functioning
         b. Using organizational procedures
         c. Using organizational ambiguity
      2. Relating to colleagues
         a. Developing a collegial network
         b. Using collegial networks
         c. Helping colleagues

      3. Planning and policy participation
        a. Using policy effectively
      4. Reaching out to client populations
        a. Determining eligibility
        b. Recording

IV. Evaluation of Professional Activities

      1. Assessing one's own intervention activities
        a. Specifying time limits for intervention
        b. Developing behavioral indicators
        c. Specifying behavior

PART TWO—FUNDAMENTAL KNOWLEDGE

I. The Cultural Context of Social Welfare and Social Work

  A. Culture
      1. Cultural relativity
      2. Cultural transitions
  B. Values
      1. Cultural values and their impact on social organization
      2. Societal values and social welfare programs
      3. Social welfare values
      4. Professional ethics
      5. Group values and behavior patterns
      6. Personal values and ethics

II. Human Functioning at the Individual, Group, and Community Levels

  A. Personal and group identity
      1. Basic human needs
      2. The human diversity continuum
      3. Human development
      4. Personality development and functioning
      5. Group development and functioning
      6. Cultural and lifestyle traditions
      7. Self-concept
      8. Group membership and identity
  B. Community
      1. Group response to need in a community
      2. Community influence and power structures
      3. Community change

III. The Social Foundations of Human Need
A. Social problems
  1. Describing social problems
  2. Major social problems
  3. Effects of social problems
  4. Social problems and social welfare services and resources
B. Social institutions
  1. Major social institutions
C. Social differentiation
  1. Social differentiation and the creation of majority-minority groups
  2. Effects of social differentiation
  3. Social differentiation and self-concept formation
  4. Social stratification and social class
D. Social power
  1. Power and social differentiation
  2. Effects of power and influence structures
  3. Power structures and the structure of social welfare services

IV. The Structure of Societal Responses to Meet Human Need
A. Social systems
  1. The structure of resource and delivery systems
  2. Comparative social welfare systems
  3. Service gaps and biases
  4. Resource information
B. Social institutions
  1. The social welfare institution
  2. Social work as a profession
C. Roles
  1. Positions and roles in groups, especially formal organizations
  2. Role performance of organizational members
D. Formal Organizations
  1. Organizations as systems
  2. Principles of organizational functioning
  3. Organizational procedures affecting formal and informal access mechanisms
  4. Organizational goals
  5. Organizational change
  6. Sources of negotiation in organizations
  7. Frameworks for organizational policy analysis
  8. Interaction and communication patterns in organizations

    9. Power relations in organizations
  10. Professional roles
  11. Employee utilization
  12. Principles of teamwork
  13. Practice objectives and service structures
  14. Consultation
  15. Professional association information
  16. Planning and carrying out membership activities

V. Strategies for Professional Intervention to Achieve Planned Change

A. Personal and social identity
    1. Self-help as helping approach
B. Teaching and learning
    1. Principles of effective teaching
    2. Teaching effectively
    3. The use of existing knowledge
    4. Planning and carrying out educational activities
C. Interpersonal influence
    1. Relationship
    2. Behavior change
    3. Intervention roles and activities
    4. Situationally specific social work intervention strategies
    5. Group communication and decisionmaking
    6. Principles of leadership
    7. Reinforcement
    8. Contracting
    9. Practice literature
D. Communication
    1. Purposes of communication
    2. Form of communication and clarity of transmission
    3. Communication within and between groups
    4. Techniques of persuasive communication
    5. Knowledge dissemination channels
    6. Influence networks
    7. Interviewing
    8. Nonverbal communication
    9. Recording
E. Social Change
    1. Problem-solving process
    2. Strategies of professional intervention
    3. Situationally specific social work intervention strategies
    4. Interventive roles and activities

      5. Policy analysis
      6. Social planning process
      7. Policy formation
      8. Citizen participation in program implementation
      9. Networks of social agencies
    10. Networks of professional organizations
    11. Self-help as a helping approach
    12. Organizing special interest groups
    13. Legislative processes
    14. Reinforcement
    15. Contracting
    16. Preparation of material for public dissemination
F. Research
      1. Problem formulation
      2. Information gathering
      3. Data collection
      4. Data analysis
      5. Organization of results
      6. Evaluative research
      7. Ethics of research with human subjects

Chapter 10

Summary and Implications

Charged with the task of strengthening baccalaureate level social work education, this project has attempted to achieve its goal in two major ways. First, the nature of entry level professional social work practice was defined and explicated, providing a picture of the end product of a baccalaureate social work curriculum. Second, the curriculum components necessary to educate the kind of practitioner described were identified, focusing particularly on knowledge, values, and skills. The process used in carrying out these activities included the involvement of social work educators, practitioners, organizational representatives, and consultants. Activities were directed and coordinated by project staff and consensus was sought to the maximum extent possible at each point in the project's work.

An earlier section of this report summarized the major issues regarding curriculum as identified by the Commission on Accreditation. This material, as well as the project findings, was utilized to identify some of the significant implications of the project's work for the future strengthening of curricula at the baccalaureate level. The implications are organized under general headings and are presented in a logical conceptual order. However, the order of presentation is only for the purpose of clarity and does not reflect any ranking in terms of significance. From the project's point of view, each of the implications is equally important.

A FOUR YEAR CURRICULUM

The curriculum content accepted as fundamental for achieving the major educational objective of accreditable baccalaureate programs—to prepare entry level professional social workers—requires a four year curriculum. The curriculum assumes close integration between social work and the liberal arts, as well as support content from the social and behavioral sciences, in order to cover all the necessary content in a planned, coherent, sequential, cumulative, nonrepetitive way. There are a number of specific implications that follow from this general point.

An integrated four year curriculum requires an interdisciplinary approach to teaching. The wide-ranging nature of the content to be covered requires the planned use of faculty expertise from other departments. It is wasteful of resources to try to teach all the content needed in the social work program itself, since the necessary resources generally exist elsewhere in the university or college. What is needed, however, are strong linkages throughout the institution, so that faculty in other departments will work with social work faculty to help achieve the program's curriculum objectives through their teaching in their courses.

In order for these linkages to flourish and be strong, at least three things must happen. The social work program must have a clear conceptualization both of its own objectives and of the curriculum content needed to achieve them. This is essential in negotiating with other departments for the coverage of needed content. Second, the social work faculty must organize its own course content so that material taken in other departments is clearly integrated into a social work frame of reference for students. Finally, the social work program must effectively utilize outreach and broker skills with other departments. The willingness to work cooperatively, to share resources, and to negotiate to achieve mutual objectives is essential. The need for these kinds of exchanges and negotiations is well illustrated in the teaching of human behavior and the social environment, human diversity, and research content, for example.

FACULTY RESOURCES

Program objectives related to practice competence require that students be properly socialized to the profession as part of their educational experience. Since students represent diverse groups, faculty resources must be adequate in terms of number and background to provide appropriate socialization opportunities. The breadth of content that a social work program must build into its curriculum exerts similar demands on faculty resources.

Most social work baccalaureate programs are small, with few faculty to carry out all program functions. Therefore, baccalaureate education generally requires nonspecialist educators who can be flexible in meeting the demands of the program. Baccalaureate education also needs faculty members from diverse groups so that the needs of diverse student populations can be met in the teaching of knowledge, values, and skills and in terms of professional socialization.

SPECIFYING ANTICIPATED PRACTICE OUTCOMES

There is, as is already well known, a distinct need for clearer specification of anticipated practice outcomes for the preparation of all entry level professional social workers. This project has elected not to attach a label to the entry level practitioner such as "generalist" or "generic," but rather to emphasize the competencies needed by the basic *social worker* in order to carry out the purpose of social work appropriate for the entry level of practice.

The project's view of social work, a view that consistently demands that the social worker relate to people within the context of their interactions with the institutions of society, has far-reaching implications. It is, for example, already evident that the entry level professional practitioner must understand the sociocultural forces that impinge on human behavior. Also urgently needed is additional content about people in the contexts of several systems that affect and influence their behavior. Content about individual and family functioning must be put in more balanced perspective by being supplemented by knowledge about groups, organizations, communities, and larger scale social processes. As will be discussed in more detail elsewhere in this chapter, cross-cultural and multicultural perspectives are also important for entry level practice.

SOCIAL WELFARE POLICY AND SERVICES CONTENT

One of the greatest weaknesses in current curricula from the point of view of the BSW practitioners with whom the project staff met was in the area of social welfare policy and services content. Project findings support this observation. While all current accredited programs include content in social welfare policy and services as part of their professional content, such content is frequently only descriptive. It does not help students with the development of a framework and skill in the use of the framework for policy analysis. In addition, project findings indicate the need for foundation content in basic economics, government, political and legislative processes, and the law.

HUMAN DIVERSITY CONTENT

As practice outcomes are more clearly specified, the place of human diversity in social work practice will also become more evident. There is a need for the reconceptualization of human diversity in general, so that it is seen as a natural and significant part of the human scene and of social work practice. Content about specific diverse groups would then be built on this base, and programs could readily concentrate on groups especially important in their geographical and service areas. However, all programs need to recognize that certain diverse groups—such as racial and ethnic minorities, women, the handicapped, the aging, and sexual preference groups—are universal and warrant inclusion no matter where the program is located.

Human diversity content cannot be dealt with in the classroom alone. The practice significance of human diversity should also be identified in field learning and in the overall educational milieu of the social work program. Such factors as the program's relationships with different parts of the community and the involvement of diverse group members in program activities (are all the secretaries women and all the faculty men?) are important aspects of the program's teaching about human diversity. This is especially the case with regard to women, who are often 75 percent or more of a program's student population. The program must create a learning milieu that is responsive to the needs of these students and that offers them appropriate learning and socialization opportunities.

RESEARCH CONTENT

Research content needs to be strengthened and more clearly focused in terms of its place in helping attain curriculum objectives. Entry level practice competence draws upon research skills in at least three ways. Students need to learn how to use appropriate research methodologies to obtain needed information, especially in small sample situations related to one's own case or other work responsibilities. Students also need the tools to be able to interpret data and other information reported in professional journals. These sources are becoming increasingly specialized and data oriented, and students must be prepared to move with them as they change. Finally, the entry level worker is beginning a professional career in social work and, as such, must have an orientation to inquiry and to contributing to the knowledge of the profession.

SPECIAL AREAS OF INTEREST

Greater clarity about practice outcomes at the entry level will allow programs to more effectively make decisions about content on special areas of interest. Once the basic curriculum is secure, and assuming that there are adequate program resources, programs can be free to meet student and faculty interests regarding special areas. Preparing students to practice in specialized service areas might be quite appropriate given a program's location and composition. Content on specialized techniques of intervention is also possible. The crucial variable is whether specialized content is consistent with the basic curriculum. If it extends and enriches the fundamental curriculum content, specialized content is appropriate; if it subverts or contradicts the basics, it is inappropriate.

PROFESSIONAL INTEGRITY

"Unlike graduate schools of social work of which almost 40 percent are located in urban centers with a population of more than 500,000, the majority, 89 (59 percent) of undergraduate social work programs are to be found in communities with 100,000 or less inhabitants. Even more interesting is the fact that of these, 70 (46 percent) are located in towns with a population of less than 50,000."[1] The preceding statement well illustrates the fact that many baccalaureate programs exist in rural and other areas where the number of social workers with sanctioned professional education is limited. There is an ongoing need to strengthen the professional identity and integrity of professional social workers practicing in these areas. They need to know how to maintain their professional ethics, how to develop a professional support network, and how to interpret professional activities and values.

EDUCATIONAL MILIEU

Currently, little attention appears to be given to the educational milieu or to the environment created for teaching and learning by the faculty, practice community, students, and others involved in the educational preparation of the entry level social worker. This project has emphasized outcomes and the competencies to be mastered if one is to function as an effective entry level practitioner. It is the conviction of this project that attention must be given to the educational milieu if the competencies, which reflect the need for a self-directed, inquiring, humane practitioner who can practice within the ethics of the profession, are to be achieved. Such professional behaviors are developed and reinforced through the educational experience.

ARTICULATION OF EDUCATIONAL LEVELS

There is an increasing need for articulation between baccalaureate and associate level programs. The growth of associate level education, especially in social work and related human service occupations, requires an appropriate response from baccalaureate educators. There is a need for collaborative activities to identify appropriate curriculum content and curriculum objectives at each level. There is also a need to develop curriculum linkages, so that students can move in an orderly way from associate level to baccalaureate programs with no loss of credits and with minimal repetition or discontinuity in curriculum content.

Additional work needs to be done in sorting out distinctions between professional identities and career lines. The differences (and similarities) between human service and mental health associate level programs on one hand and baccalaureate social work programs on the other need to be clarified. Curriculum objectives and content need to reflect this clarification, and employing agencies should be helped to develop appropriate expections and job opportunities for graduates from these different programs. Meanwhile, the continuation of ongoing efforts to further clarify linkages between baccalaureate and graduate education is also important.

CONCLUSION

The implications of the work of this project are far reaching and, we believe, significant. In recognition of the great responsibility that this project has carried for the future development of social work education, we, the project staff, have attempted to work carefully, responsibly, and collaboratively with our education and practice colleagues. We know that there are weaknesses and gaps in our work—limited time, resources, and energy have made them unavoidable. But we also believe that there are great strengths and that this project makes it possible for social work education to move ahead with a clearer purpose and from a sounder base. We earnestly hope that our profession can continue the momentum begun by this project and that it will continue to improve professional practice by further strengthening all levels of professional education.

NOTES

1. Alfred Stamm, *An Analysis of Undergraduate Social Work Programs Approved by CSWE, 1971* (New York: Council on Social Work Education, 1971), p. 20.

Appendixes

Introduction

There are three appendixes to this report, each of which contains information that supplements the main body of the report in a significant way. Placement of material in the appendixes does not indicate its relative lack of significance, but rather, the organizational need to maintain the flow and continuity between the sections of the report that comprise its main body. Appendix materials, while important to the achievement of the objectives of the project, serve to enrich and elaborate on the earlier parts of the project report. Each of the three appendixes will be described in turn.

The first, Appendix A, consists of four papers commissioned by the project. Each author was selected by the project for his acknowledged expertise in a particular area. Each paper addresses a significant issue for baccalaureate level social work education, exploring the dimensions of the issue and suggesting possibilities for resolving it. Each issue has direct implications for entry level practice, and for the design of baccalaureate curricula to prepare entry level professional practitioners.

1. "Professional Values and Professional Ethics in Social Work Education," by Frank Loewenberg, dean of the School of Social Work, Bar-Ilan University, Israel. This paper addresses the place of values and ethics in baccalaureate social work education. Problems encountered in teaching values and ethics are discussed, along with educational strategies that may allow for more effective teaching in this area in the future.

109

2. "Educational Milieu as Curriculum," by Tom Walz, dean of the School of Social Work, University of Iowa. The concept of curriculum as including all of the learning experiences that a student has while participating in the total environment of the social work program is presented in this paper. The environment is broken down into its component parts, and each is analyzed to determine how it can contribute to the objectives of the program.

3. "Bureaucratic Functioning as a Social Work Skill," by Robert Pruger, School of Social Welfare, University of California at Berkeley. While most baccalaureate social work educators recognize that the ability of practitioners to function is heavily influenced by their ability to effectively use the organizations in which they work, there has been little success in identifying strategies to improve the organizational effectiveness of social workers. This paper attempts to identify some of the major obstacles to organizational effectiveness, as well as several strategies for overcoming them. Implications for curriculum content are also addressed.

4. "Social Work in Governmental Agencies," by Edward Weaver, executive director of the American Public Welfare Association. This paper begins by reviewing the past utilization of baccalaureate social workers in governmental agencies. Current utilization patterns are then described, along with the implications for curriculum content of changing roles of baccalaureate social workers in governmental agencies.

Appendix B, "Knowledge, Values, and Skills Essential for the Attainment of the Baccalaureate Level Competencies: A Complete Elaboration," accomplishes two major tasks. The first is the listing of fundamental knowledge and skill curriculum content organized by competency. This illustrates the way in which the knowledge and skill curriculum content was derived from the competencies. In the main body of the report (Chapter 9), the knowledge and skill content is listed without references to specific competencies in order to avoid repetition and so that the knowledge and skills can be organized in a clear conceptual way. The second purpose of Appendix B is to provide full details and a complete elaboration of knowledge and skill categories that are summarized in Chapter 9.

The project hopes that Appendixes A and B will be helpful to baccalaureate social work educators as they continue the ongoing effort to strengthen entry level professional social work education. The issues addressed in Appendix A may be useful when formulating program and curriculum objectives and when attempting to decide on the most effective program structure, teaching methods, and curriculum content. Appendix B should be useful for selecting and organizing curriculum objectives and content. However, it should be remembered that the knowledge and skills elaborated in this appendix represent the basics, or fundamentals, for the preparation of the entry level professional practitioner. It is assumed that each program will build and elaborate on the basics in a manner appropriate to its particular objectives, needs, and resources.

Finally, Appendix C is a listing of all of the persons who have contributed to the work of this project. Some reacted to drafts of project documents, and others provided their views on various practice and curriculum issues. Still others provided informal consultation to project staff or served in some other way. Some did many of these things. But regardless of the specific activity, each person helped to make this project, and this project report, better than it would otherwise have been. The project staff are deeply grateful to each person for his or her help and support.

Appendix A

Position Papers on Issues of Significance to Social Work Education

Professional Values and Professional Ethics in Social Work Education

Frank M. Loewenberg

INTRODUCTION: VALUES IN SOCIAL WORK PRACTICE AND EDUCATION

In the development of the professions, values have always occupied a crucial role, and social workers have stressed the value base of their profession since the earliest days of the profession. They have maintained that their practice is based on a combination of three elements—skills, knowledge, and values—and among these, values is generally considered preeminent.[1] Mature professions, argues Bartlett (1970:63), rests on "strong bodies of knowledge and values from which scientific and ethical principles that guide the operation of the practitioner are derived." Mukandaroa (1968:141) is not the only one who has suggested that the uniqueness of social work derived neither from its knowledge base nor from the specialized expertise of the practitioners, but from the profession's values, which give "a sense of purpose and direction" to social work practice.

There is wide consensus about those values that provide the basis for social work practice. Differences and problems begin to arise only when social workers or theorists attempt to operationalize these abstract and generalized values. Unfortunately, the generalized values about which there is agreement do not provide specific normative referents and are not sufficiently useful to serve as guides for appropriate practice behaviors. But professional values have real meaning only when they provide "governance and guidance for action" (Perlman, 1976:382). As long as values remain nonspecific and do not offer such guidance, workers may engage in a variety of different or even contradictory activities while claiming support from the same value. Only those values that are specifically defined in action terms are helpful for practitioners.

The dominant place of values in social work makes it essential that social work educators pay attention to values, including their clarification and operationalization, as well as their transmission to students. Value education in the professional curriculum must not be left to chance. It is (or should be) a matter of high priority to define those professional values that students must acquire before they begin to practice. The most effective ways for teaching these values must also be identified. Pumphrey (1959:13) noted in the landmark curriculum study that the area of values was frequently omitted "from specific compilations of essential learning components." Fifteen years later, Vigilante (1974:108) also observed that "values have received only superficial attention from scholars, theory builders, and curriculum designers."

Despite near universal agreement on their importance, social work educators have not found it easy to include values in the curriculum. They cite one or more of the following reasons for this:

1. Defining professional values is not the job of educators. As long as practitioners have not clearly identified professional values, there is a danger that the values selected by the faculty may not be congruent with those held by the professional community. In medicine, for example, it was noted that the values of medical school faculties often ran counter to those of practitioners (Funkenstein, 1958).

2. Most academicians avoid the study of values, arguing that a scientific discipline should not be based on beliefs that are scientifically untestable. Further, these academicians contend, since values are not empirically demonstrable, it is not possible to achieve agreement on an appropriate set of values for any given field (Page, 1977:49). Though some social work educators may reject these contentions, they are not entirely comfortable about including values as a separate curriculum element.

3. Others argue that the explication and specification of professional values requires a more fully developed knowledge and theory base than is presently available in social work. Until this occurs, there is a tendency to overemphasize values to substitute for the underdeveloped knowledge and theory base. This in turn makes it difficult to study values in the serious, balanced, and objective way that they deserve (Vigilante, 1974).

4. The teachability of values is controversial. Many agree with the

maxim that "values are caught, not taught." Feldman and New-comb (1970), after examining 1,500 empirical studies of the impact of college on value changes, reported some positive findings, though the degree and nature of these differed in various colleges and curricula. Similarly, four of the five studies of graduate social work education reported either a negative outcome or no impact on changing students' values (Varley, 1963 and 1968; Hayes and Varley, 1965; Brown, 1970); only Sharwell (1974) reported certain positive findings.

The place of values in the professional curriculum, important as it may be, is problematic. The mere acknowledgement of the value base is certainly not sufficient. As Perlman (1976:381) wrote, "A value has small worth except as it is moved or is movable, from believing into doing, from verbal affirmation into action." Values that do not lead to desired behaviors are useless. But most values are stated on so high and generalized a level that they do not lead to' such behavior. Generally it is necessary and desirable to deduce ethical principles from the values, and these, when stated as professional ethics, can provide guides for practitioner behavior.

PROFESSIONAL ETHICS: VALUES IN ACTION

Professional ethics have been called "values in action" or "values in operation" (Levy, 1976:233 and 14). They represent behavioral expectations or preferences that provide the practitioner with a guide for his or her professional conduct. Social work ethics provide the social worker with a set of guides or principles that can be applied in practice.

Every significant group develops a formal or informal system of ethics to guide relationships within the group and between group members and outsiders. Professional ethics serve an additional function since they are designed to protect clients and potential consumers of services who have no way of evaluating the competence and integrity of those who present themselves as professionals. Thus Greenwood (1957), in his classic article on the social work profession, observed that the ethical code of every professional group can be described in terms of colleague-colleague and professional-client relations.

Professional ethics describe ideal or preferred professional behavior patterns and not the personal qualities of the practitioner. The ethics are derived from those values that social workers have traditionally identified as professional values, but they are expressed in action terms. While values are concerned with what is *good*, ethics are generally more concerned with what is *right*. The reason for including ethics in the professional curriculum is not to give the student a number of ethical prescriptions that will prescribe his or her behavior in every foreseeable problem situation, but rather to help students learn to apply these ethical principles to any new situations they may face, situations that no one today can predict. Traditionally, professional ethics were not taught. They were assimilated by watching a master practitioner perform. This apprentice model of transmiting professional ethics was satisfactory as long as the new practitioner faced only situations similar to those faced by his or her master. But today, when radically new conditions are commonplace, every practitioner must be able to apply and utilize the basic ethical principles, no matter what the situation. Today, it is not possible to depend only on modeling for the effective transmission of professional ethics. The world has become too complicated to leave the learning of professional ethics to chance. They should be incorporated systematically into the professional curriculum.

Code of Social Work Ethics and Social Work Practice

Social workers need a statement of ethical principles or a code of ethics to guide their professional behavior because of the high degree of ambiguity that characterizes the situations in which they work. A contemporary code of professional ethics must provide guidance for a world that is characterized by change and uncertainty. Such a code generally is not based on legal enforcement or police power, but rather on the informed consensus of professional colleagues.

The utilization of written codes to regulate professional conduct is not a recent innovation. Nearly 4,000 years ago Hammurabi attempted to control the practice of Babylonian physicians through a code of laws and principles. Hippocrates' oath was meant to guide the professional conduct of Greek doctors and has come down to this day as a significant and powerful code of professional ethics. The first of the modern professional ethical codes was said to have been prepared by Thomas Percival (1803) for the physicians and surgeons connected with the Manchester Infirmary. The American Medical Association's first code of ethics (1847) was most probably based on Percival's code. But a general interest in developing codes of ethics did not occur among American professional groups until after the First World War. The May 1922 issue of *The Annals of the American Society of Political and Social Sciences* was devoted entirely to the subject of ethical codes in the professions and in business. Contemporary observers viewed the publication of this volume of the prestigious *Annals* as the trigger event in the modern history of codes of professional ethics (Elliott, 1931).

Two veteran social workers, Mary Van Kleeck and Graham R. Taylor, prepared an article on the development of professional standards in social work for this volume of *The Annals*. They noted that social work did not have a written code of professional ethics, but that social workers nevertheless were guided by the ideal of service rather than by any thought of pecuniary gain. In the years following the appearance of *The Annals*, a number of attempts were made to produce a written code of social work ethics. Thus, in 1923, the American Association for Organizing Family Social Work discussed (but did not adopt) a code with thirty-eight paragraphs. Many of the items in this code are found in subsequent codes and still sound familiar to present day social workers (e.g., "The social worker's first duty is toward his clients, unless the performance of this duty jeopardizes the welfare of the community"). A year later the American Association of Social Workers appointed a National Committee on Professional Ethics. Many local AASW chapters discussed the need for a code of ethics, and some produced draft documents. In 1924, the Toledo chapter became the first to publicize such a draft code of ethical principles. Even though this brief code contained only very general principles, it spurred other chapters to produce their own versions.

This is not the place to detail the subsequent history of the development of the code of ethics. Suffice it to say that the delegate assembly of the National Association of Social Workers adopted a code in 1960 and amended this code in 1967. The code has received a mixed response from practitioners. Recently Levy (1976:115) wrote that this code "is far from definitive and it is still in the stage of emergence." Nevertheless, a code of professional ethics does exist, and those responsible for the preparation of new social workers must take seriously their responsibility to introduce the neophyte to it.

At the time of this writing, the NASW Task Force on Ethics has prepared a proposal for a revised code of ethics.* The task force noted that the proposed revision sought to remain within the spirit and general intent of the original code because that document encompassed a basically sound and durable set of principles. The basic professional values remain unchanged, but the world has changed so

---

*At the delegate assembly in 1977 the proposed revision was returned to the committee for revision and future action.

that the application of these basic values requires updated guidelines. The task force reemphasized the special importance of professional ethics for social workers: "To a greater degree than is true of other professions, the issues with which social work deals are by nature ambiguous. Because of the peculiar mix of moral and technical elements in social work practice, professional ethics must have a central place in the ongoing activities of social workers."

Major Social Work Ethics in the Social Work Curriculum

The rationale for including social work ethics in the curriculum (the *why*) was discussed earlier; in a later section we will discuss some of the educational problems and suggest techniques for teaching social work ethics (the *how*). Here we will attempt to focus on the content that may be appropriate for inclusion in the undergraduate professional social work curriculum (the *what*).

Every social work student must become familiar with the profession's code of ethics. The failure of many social work practice texts to explicitly mention the code of ethics is unfortunate. It is simply not sufficient that students internalize a set of behaviors appropriate for the problems they face today; tomorrow they may face situations for which they have no prepared behavioral response. If a code of professional ethics has been internalized so that it can be applied to a variety of different situations, any new problem condition should not present any unusual difficulties.

The specific provisions found in a code of professional ethics for social workers differ from time to time, but an inspection of many of the codes drawn up over the past half century indicates that the following basic elements are found in nearly all. These are the basic social work ethical principles that every student must learn to utilize when making practice decisions.

1. Giving priority to the needs and well-being of clients(s)-consumer(s) over the worker's personal interests and over the agency's organizational interests. Neither the interests, conveniences, and needs of the worker nor the structure and goals of the agency should determine the nature and direction of the social worker's intervention. Instead, the needs and well-being of the client(s)-consumer(s) must be the primary criteria for determining the most effective social intervention strategy. If the worker cannot engage in what is best for the client-consumer (due to his own limitations, agency structure or budget, or any other reason) he or she must refer the client-consumer to the organization that can best serve him or her.

2. Providing services without discrimination, and conducting oneself impartially with all individuals and groups who request service or seek help. This impartiality and the willingness to work with everybody characterizes the professional and distinguishes him or her from other do-gooders. The professional social worker cannot and need not be "like" the client-consumer, but he or she must be ready to provide service to all without discrimination. A corollary of this principle suggests that every social worker must deal with those elements in society that continue to violate the law by discriminating and preventing others from gaining access to opportunities for self-realization.

3. Practicing in a way that respects every individual and group's right to their own lifestyle. Even while social workers must be clear about their own values, they must be openminded to the opinions of others and must respect points of view other than their own. This ethic is not identical with the principle of client self-determination, and contemporary social workers have recognized that in fact there are limitations to this principle. Nevertheless, we should take note of Towle's comment (1965:18) that "the client's right to self-determination was one of the first, if not the first, of our beliefs to become a banner around which we rallied." The right of clients or consumers to their own lifestyles includes the right to terminate the social intervention engagement at any time they choose.

4. Accepting responsibility for professional activities and becoming accountable for them to clients or consumers, the agency, professional colleagues, and the community. Professional responsibility can be realized only when every professional becomes accountable for his or her practice.

5. Practicing competently and with integrity. Service must be provided on a superior level, utilizing the most advanced professional knowledge, skills, and values. Intervention activities should never be based on impulse or happenstance, but must reflect the competence and integrity of the practitioner.

6. Contributing to the development of social work knowledge. Knowledge building and theory development must not be limited to a small group of ivory tower specialists, but require the participation of every professional practitioner. Knowledge building is not an activity that stands apart from practice. Instead, social workers should utilize practice in such a way that they can contribute to the development of new knowledge and insight.

7. Protecting the community against unethical practices in the social work field. The colleague relationship does not supercede accountability to clients and consumers and to the community. Since an

outsider will find it difficult to assess social work practice and to identify unethical practices, professionals carry a particular responsibility for protecting those who require social work services.

While these seven ethical principles represent the profession's approach to serving people responsibly, equitably, and effectively, there is an additional area that is receiving increased recognition as being of major concern to social work. Social workers often work with involuntary clients and other client groups subject to explicit social control mechanisms, such as infants for whom adoption is sought, persons in the criminal justice system, and persons in residential institutions of many kinds (such as mental hospitals, facilities for the developmentally disabled). These clients pose especially difficult ethical issues for social workers, since many ethical principles of the profession cannot be applied (respecting lifestyles and giving priority to the needs and well-being of clients, for example). In these instances, the social worker is confronted with difficult and often painful decisions regarding how to act ethically in situations that prevent the application of the usual ethical principles.

This suggests that part of the skill of the competent social worker is being able to deal with situations where value conflicts are created by ethical ambiguity or violation. It is not uncommon for social welfare program regulations or agency procedures to be incompatible with the ethical principles of the profession. Therefore, the social worker must know more than the ethics of the profession—he or she must also know how to deal with situations in which ethical issues are unusually complex and difficult. Working with some categories of involuntary clients illustrates the problem. What is ethical behavior in a mental hospital when the client's privacy, right to confidentiality, and right to live a chosen although controversial lifestyle (such as transvesticism) are violated?

The profession itself has not yet found solutions to these kinds of situations, so definitive solutions cannot be presented here. However, any curriculum to prepare competent social work practitioners must address this problem if its educational content in the area of values and ethics is to be realistic and appropriate. Each program will discuss its own set of strategies to deal with the problem, but at least the student will be prepared to deal thoughtfully and responsibly with problems of acting ethically when they arise.*

*The preceding three paragraphs were written by project staff and are included with Dr. Loewenberg's permission.

TEACHING SOCIAL WORK ETHICS:
ISSUES AND CHALLENGES

Socializing social work students to professional ethics should be a priority objective of the social work curriculum. However, this objective may face two obstacles in a university where the emphasis usually is placed on knowledge and theory development. There are the academic purists who deny that socialization to the professional ethics is a proper function for university educators. And there are the academic ritualists who accept this function, but who argue that the mere transmission of knowledge about ethics is sufficient. Neither contention is valid. Professional education, no matter where it is offered, must concern itself with socialization to the professional ethics, with skill development, and with knowledge transmission; any one or two of these elements will not be sufficient to adequately prepare the new professional worker.

A problem of a different kind is the tendency to overemphasize the importance of the teacher in this teaching and socialization process. Only rarely does the influence of a teacher result in significant changes in his or her students. Thus, rather than relying on individual example, teachers should attempt to structure learning conditions and create situations that will enhance learning and foster the internalization of the professional ethics. Since the acquisition of ethics usually is not brought about item by item, the teacher should attempt to utilize the total learning and living environment. Conditions and situations that are conducive to achieving this objective include:

1. new situations in which the student cannot cope using only his or her present knowledge and behavioral guides;
2. situations characterized by conflicting demands or cross-pressures arising out of social inconsistencies for which the student's present knowledge and behavioral guides are inadequate;
3. conditions where the student must associate with people who uiltize entirely different behavioral guides, particularly when the student's own reference group is far away or prescribes norms that are not relevant in the present situation.

It is the structuring of these situations, and not the mere teaching of theoretical knowledge or abstract practice skills, that may result in value and ethics changes.

Though changes are usually desired, there are students whose current values and ethics need not be changed. However, unless they are reinforced, these desirable values might turn to other, less desirable ones. If reinforcement of the existing values is the objective, teachers should attempt to structure situations so that they are not novel and so that they will not present the student with conflicting demands or cross-pressures. Every attempt should also be made for these students to associate with peers who think and believe as they do.

Values and the Teaching of Professional Ethics

No student comes to social work education without values. Generally, students bring a set of basic values that is more or less in consonance with societal values. Professional social work values are derived from these same societal values. However, though deriving from the same source, there may be differences in priorities, intensities, and applications between any given student's values and those of the profession.

One of the characteristics of American society is its tolerance of diversity. Conflicts and incongruencies that arise out of this diversity are, within fixed limits, sanctioned and even institutionalized. Thus, in the American value set, it is possible to find an acceptable countervalue for almost every basic value. Often value and countervalue appear side by side and have *equal* validity. The basic value of "the importance of the individual" competes with the countervalue of "the importance of the group (or the community)." Though different students will attach differing emphasis to this value and its countervalue, it is improbable that a student raised in American (or in any Western) society will reject either of these two value positions out of hand. Social work ethics also include this value and its countervalue (though not necessarily with the identical emphasis). It will be possible to socialize students to the professional social work ethic with relative ease because they internalized a common value base even before coming in contact with social work education. On the other hand, our experience with recent immigrants from the USSR suggests that students raised in a value system that is entirely different from that of the West will have great difficulty in becoming socialized to social work ethics. For example, a student raised in a society that does not accept the worth and inherent dignity of every individual as a basic value, but who instead has internalized a prior and exclusive commitment to the state or to the collective, will find it very difficult to accept the social work ethic that demands giving priority to the needs of the individual client.

Theoretical and empirical evidence suggests that regardless of the change technique used, basic values rarely change among young adults and adults. But if the basic value set of the learner is compatible with the profession's values, change, especially change in operational values and in the professional ethics that guide behavior, is possible. This is the reason why a social work curriculum that focuses on professional ethics can have an impact on a bigoted student who grew up in an environment where the worth and the inherent dignity of some (but not all) individuals was valued. Given favorable conditions, such a student may be able to adopt a professional ethic that proscribes all forms of discrimination and bigotry.

Educational Millieu: The Crucial Factor
In Education

The decisive influence of the environment on human behavior has been well established. Perhaps less appreciated is the crucial influence of the environment on learning. Earlier we noted that one of the principal functions of social work teachers was to structure the learning environment to facilitate the acquisition and internalization of professional ethics. Two principal ways come to mind in which faculty members can be instrumental in creating a favorable learning environment—one of these relates to the teachers, the other, to the students.

Even though a number of research studies have found that teachers do not have a large influence on students, this need not be so if teachers become more skillful in taking advantage of student-teacher interaction opportunities. The information available suggests that chances for successful influencing increase when a teacher is honest and authentic, makes herself or himself available to students outside of the classroom, and risks himself or herself in situations similar to those in which students are expected to risk themselves. The teacher who meets these requirements will have a better chance of serving as a role model. And though the expert role model, located outside of the peer culture, cannot alone generate value and ethics changes, she or he can have great influence.

A second way in which the faculty can increase the curriculum's impact on students is by agreeing on the desirable and essential professional ethics. The general tendency to select people with similar values and attitudes as friends and associates holds also for faculty advisors. If there are wide divergencies and differences on the question of professional ethics among faculty members, students will tend to ignore messages and suggestions from teachers with a professional ethics stance that differs from their own. They will select faculty members with an ethics stance similar to their own, in order to receive support and reinforcement for their present mode of operation. The inability to find such faculty reinforcements for undesirable ethics will facilitate change in the desired direction.

Far more important than the faculty is the crucial role of the peer group. As long as the peer group supports a certain behavior, undesirable as it may be, the faculty will have little impact on changing it. Student recruitment and selection provides the faculty with some influence on the composition of the peer group. By aggressively recruiting some and not others, by accepting some applicants and rejecting others, the faculty has an opportunity to determine the composition of the student body. This student body will before long become a significant peer group and a powerful tool in achieving change. Faculty members, therefore, must take seriously their responsibilities in student recruitment and selection.

Classroom Education and Professional Ethics

It has been customary in many circles to belittle the role of the classroom in education for the professions. Yet this is an educational arena that must not be overlooked. The objective of classroom instruction in education for professional ethics is not to anticipate every possible problem that students will encounter in their subsequent professional career but to provide students with the tools they need to handle these problems when they do encounter them. The goal should not be achieving the widest possible coverage but giving students sufficient experience in the application and adaptation of what they have learned. Knowing that individuals will innovate and change only when they encounter problems for which their present coping techniques are inadequate, it is the classroom teacher's responsibility to present his or her students with a succession of new challenges that will stimulate the desired responses. Lectures, quite obviously, are not sufficient to achieve these goals. The active involvement of students in problem solving is essential even in the classroom if change is really desired.

Field Instruction and Education for Professional Ethics

Talking about what is expected of students is not nearly as effective as giving students the opportunity to practice the expected behaviors. While lectures may be effective in transmiting certain types of information, they are not effective in bringing about behavior changes. Student activity, particularly opportunities to test newly learned ethics and different behavior styles, is much more effective. In the field, it is possible to structure new situations so that students will abandon previous coping mechanisms and adopt new ones. Teachers and field instructors would be derelict if they did not present their students with people and groups whose behaviors, lifestyles, and problems are quite different from those with which they have been accustomed to work in the past. It is precisely these types of new experiences that will facilitate the testing and adoption of professional ethics.

The importance of the field faculty in professional education was noted by Merton et al. (1957), who found that medical school students chose practicing physicians rather than classroom teachers as models. Similarly, the social work teacher who is completely removed from the practice world is likely to have less of an impact on students than a colleague who remains in active contact with the practice field. Beyond the personal impact of any given faculty member, there is the question of the relevancy and connectedness of the curriculum and of the learning experiences to the actual practice situation. The real world is more exciting and makes more of an impact than any artificial arrangement.

IN CONCLUSION

Although values and ethics have always been an important part of social work, the complexities and rapid changes that characterize contemporary society make them especially important for the practitioner of today and tomorrow. While the knowledge and skill foundations of professional practice are becoming stronger, they must not overshadow the ethical framework that guide their use. The baccalaureate social work curriculum must include content appropriate to the profession's code of ethics. However, it should also provide the ground work for dealing with situations of ethical conflict and ambiguity, such as are typically faced when working with involuntary clients.

How values and ethics are best transmited is a question that has evaded definitive answers in spite of the profession's historical concern with them. Several specific strategies for the teaching and reinforcing of values and ethics are discussed in this paper, and throughout there is the implicit point that each part of the curriculum—the classroom, the field, peer interaction, and student-faculty contact—must be consistent in its approach to values and ethics. In values and ethics content, as in any other curriculum content, there is no substitute for the use of carefully structured learning experiences in order to achieve curriculum and program objectives.

NOTES

1. There are many definitions of the term *value*. Perhaps the simplest is that proposed by Bartlett (1970:63), who wrote that values "refer to what is regarded as good and desirable." Using a more scholarly language, Kluckhohn (1951:395) defined value as "a conception, explicit or implicit, distinctive of an individual or characteristic of a group, of the desirable which influences the selection from available modes, means, and ends of action." Williams (1967:23) similarly defined values as "those conceptions of desirable states of affairs that are utilized in selective conduct for preference or choice or as justification for proposed or actual behavior."

BIBLIOGRAPHY

Barnsley, John H. 1972. *The Social Reality of Ethics: The Comparative Analysis of Moral Codes.* London: Routledge & Kegan Paul.

Bartlett, Harriet M. 1970. *The Common Base of Social Work Practice.* New York: National Association of Social Workers.

Barton, Allen H. 1959. *Studying the Effects of College Education.* New Haven, Conn.: Hazen Foundation.

Biesteck, Felix P. 1965. "Some Problems in Identifying the Values of the Social Work Profession." In *Ethics and Values in Social Work,* pp. 3–15. Chicago: School of Social Work, Loyola University.

Bliss, Brian P., and Alan G. Johnson. 1975. *Aims and Motives in Clinical Medicine: A Practical Approach to Medical Ethics.* London: Pitman.

Brown, Malcolm J. 1970. "Social Work Values in a Developing Country." *Social Work* 15 (January): 107–12.

Clark, Burton R. 1956. "Organizational Adaptation and Precarious Values." *American Sociological Review* 21:327–36.

Elliott, Lula J. 1931. *Social Work Ethics.* New York: American Association of Social Workers.

Feldman, Kenneth A., and Theodore M. Newcomb. 1970. *The Impact of College on Students.* San Francisco: Jossey-Bass.

Funkenstein, Daniel. 1958. "The Implications of Diversity." In *The Ecology of Medical Students,* eds. Helen Gee and Robert Glaser. Evanston: Association of American Medical Colleges.

Greenwood, Ernest. 1957. "Attributes of a Profession." *Social Work* 2 (July):45–55.

Hayes, Dorothy D., and Barbara K. Varley. 1965. "The Impact of Social Work Education on Students' Values." *Social Work* 10 (July):40–46.

Jacob, Philip E. 1957. *Changing Values in College.* New York: Harper & Brothers.

Kluckhohn, Clyde. 1951. "Values and Value-Orientation in the Theory of Action: An Exploration in Definition and Classification." In *Towards a General Theory of Action,* eds. Talcott Parsons and Edward A. Shils, pp. 388–433. Cambridge Mass.: Harvard University Press.

Levy, Charles S. 1973. "The Value Base of Social Work." *Journal for Education of Social Work* 9 (Winter):34–42.

―――. 1976. *Social Work Ethics.* New York: Human Sciences Press.

Loewenberg, Frank M. 1977. *Fundamentals of Social Intervention.* New York: Columbia University Press.

MacIver, Robert. 1955. "The Social Significance of Professional Ethics." *The Annals of the American Academy of Political Science* 297 (January):118–24.

Merton, Robert K.; George G. Reader; and Patricia L. Kendall, eds. 1957. *The Student-Physician: Introductory Studies in the Sociology of Medical Education.* Cambridge, Mass.: Harvard University Press.

Mukandaroa, K. 1968. "Modes of Professional Education: Functions of Field Learning in the Curriculum." *Tulane Studies in Social Welfare* 11 (February).

Page, Alfred N. 1977. "Economics and Social Work: A Neglected Relationship." *Social Work* 22:48–53.

Perlman, Helen Harris. 1976. "Believing and Doing: Values in Social Work Education." *Social Casework* 57:381–90.

Pumphrey, Muriel W. 1959. *The Teaching of Values and Ethics in Social Work Education* (Curriculum Study, vol. xiii). New York: Council on Social Work Education.

Sharwell, George R. 1974. "Can Values Be Taught?" *Journal of Education for Social Work* 10 (Spring):99–105.

Towle, Charlotte. 1965. "Ethics and Values in Social Work." In *Ethics and Values in Social Work*, pp. 17–24. Chicago: School of Social Work, Loyola University.

Varley, Barbara K. 1963. "Socialization in Social Work Education." *Social Work* (July):102–109.

―――. 1968. "Social Work Values: Change in Value Commitments of Students from Admission to MSW Graduation." *Journal of Education for Social Work* 4 (Fall):67–76.

Vigilante, Joseph L. 1974. "Between Values and Science: Education for the Profession during a Model Crisis *or* is Proof Truth." *Journal of Education for Social Work* 10 (Fall):107–15.

Williams, Robin M. Jr. 1967. "Individual and Group Values." *The Annals* 371:20–37.

Educational Milieu as Curriculum

Thomas Walz

TOWARD A DEFINITION

To most faculty, curriculum is something we associate with what we teach, how we teach, and when we teach. The formal definition would be that curriculum is the structure, organization, sequencing, and content of a particular field of knowledge. By whatever definition, however, curriculum is a fairly broad concept. Unfortunately, many faculty are inclined to not take advantage of its breadth and to limit curriculum to something directly related to "a course or a program of courses." This predilection for exclusively viewing curriculum as "course-related activities" produces some costly oversights, and some of the most exciting and vital components of the educational experience are missed.

In this paper we offer a somewhat expanded definition of curriculum by including the concept of "educational milieu"[1] as a component of curriculum and by making educational milieu an important objective in curriculum building and curriculum enrichment. It will be argued that the conscious development of a strong, positive educational milieu is necessary for building a quality undergraduate social work program. The route to vitality, energy, and creativity in a social work program is through developing a strong and positive educational milieu.

This chapter is organized to provide: (1) a definition of educational milieu, (2) an outline of the educational goals around which an undergraduate social work educational milieu could be designed,

131

and (3) a theoretical framework for analyzing educational milieu for the purpose of implementing the concept within an undergraduate social work program.

In general terms, educational milieu can be defined as the totality of an educational experience or the sum of all factors and forces that bear upon the teaching and learning process. Educational milieu, accordingly, includes all of the incidental and background factors that shape the educational process and product, as well as the process-product itself. To speak of educational milieu is to speak of an educational gestalt: the fit and complementarity of those factors that come together to form an educational statement.

Marshall McLuhan identified the educational principle behind the concept of educational milieu in the now worn aphorism "the media is the message."[2] Based on this principle, the educational process is inseparable from the educational product—the two coalesce into one.

Milieu, according to Webster's dictionary, is defined as "surrounding or environment." Webster unfortunately would have us think of the educational environment as separable from the educational product. We would prefer to think of educational milieu as a "filled" environment, not some sort of backdrop to or stage for education. We take the position that educational milieu has definite "content." It conveys an educational message as readily as a classroom lecture.

There is a useful analog for grasping the nature and meaning of educational milieu with which most social worker educators are familiar. We refer to the theory of milieu therapy introduced into residential and institutional care of the emotionally ill some years ago.[3] Milieu therapy shifted attention to a new set of factors within an institutional environment that seemed to affect the well-being of patients. For sometime, therapy had been felt to be principally, if not exclusively, a function of the professional activities of a few well-trained, high status therapists in a treatment setting. The new factors considered to affect the therapeutic well-being of patients included the nonprofessional support staff, the ward-hospital administrative practices (rules and regulations), the physical attributes and arrangements of the ward-hospital, and even the community outreach and community relations of the hospital toward the outside world. What the new theory of therapeutic milieu did was to enlarge the therapeutic field by arguing the importance of many additional features of organizational life that professional ethnocentrism had rendered invisible in the past. By analogy, we would expect educational milieu to lead us in the same direction, into the exploration of the role of the nonacademic personnel, of the administrative policies and practices of our programs, and of the physical dimension of the educational setting and its community interface as having direct curriculum impact. Our theoretical framework for analyzing the concept of educational milieu is based on these (and other) factors.

EDUCATIONAL MILIEU FOR WHAT

Central in curriculum building is the issue of what is to be taught, or, as one writer put it, "What's worth knowing."[4] Building an educational milieu within an undergraduate social work program means being explicit about what kind of an educational milieu is desired. What educational statements do we want expressed or reinforced through milieu. Whether we consciously build these statements or not, the educational milieu conveys educational messages to those who experience our program. To a certain extent, the educational milieu will be shaped by accreditation standards—the minimal expectations of what should be learned within a program. Beyond this, however, the educational program expresses its uniqueness and personality by affording its own special educational experience for its students through its educational milieu.

The content of educational milieu can be best expressed through educational orientations or themes. Each program needs to define its own set of orientations and to mold its milieu to express them. One undergraduate social work program,[5] for example, has established its milieu-building orientations as follows:

1. a humanistic orientation that expresses the caring and concern of a helping profession;
2. a cross-cultural orientation that stresses the basic equality of all persons, while appreciating and respecting cultural difference;
3. an international orientation that places a special focus on the needs and development of third world peoples;
4. a multidisciplinary orientation that acknowledges the varied sources of knowledge and assumes a shared role with other professionals in the provision of social services;
5. a postindustrial orientation that explores the full range of tools and technological developments in terms of their contribution to improved social functioning;
6. an alternative futures and social development orientation that critically assesses the new technology and searches for alternative ways of enhancing human social functioning;

7. an ecological orientation that stresses the interdependency of persons within a natural environment;
8. a community-based orientation that encourages full involvement of the educational program in the affairs of the community and the profession.

This is but a sample of the possible educational orientations around which an undergraduate social work educational milieu conceivably could be designed. These articulations are broad general statements, out of which course structures can be defined, administrative decisions shaped, faculty and students selected, the physical facility designed, and so forth. It is from these educational orientations, expressed through the educational milieu, that an educational program derives its character and its personality.

ANALYTIC FRAMEWORK

To build an educational milieu, however, it is necessary to have more than a definition and a direction. One must also understand the analytic components, the building blocks, of the concept. Unfortunately, educational milieu as a curriculum concept has received scant attention in the literature of educational theory, though John Dewey, Harold Taylor, and others wrote strongly about the informal learning that takes place beyond the classroom. Hence, we felt it necessary to provide a conceptualization of educational milieu that could serve as a guide to faculty and program administrators in building their preferred educational milieu.[6]

Since there already exists adequate conceptualization of curriculum in terms of course-related activities, the theoretical framework for analyzing educational milieu will be limited to the "surroundings or environment" factors. With this in mind, we offer the following as added components of curriculum-milieu:

1. The Educational Space, or the arena within which the educational experience takes place;
2. The Physical Place, or the architectural features of the educational setting built by individuals;
3. The Human Social Network, or the persons, academic and non-academic, who make up the educational enterprise in a personal sense;
4. The Administrative Policy and Procedural Arrangements, or the process by which educational resources are allocated and educational decisions are made;
5. The Modeling Behaviors of the School and Its Representatives,

or the fit and complementarity of actual behavior to educational
goals and objectives;
6. The Educational Gestalt, or the fit and complementarity of all
of the above—their integration—in terms of giving definition to
an educational milieu.

Each of these components will be discussed with a view toward
how they might be implemented in an undergraduate social work
educational program.

Educational Space
Educational space refers to the location(s) of learning. In this
context, educational milieu building requires that attention be paid
to the geography of teaching and learning, which includes classroom
space, a program or school space, a college or university space, a
social agency space, and a community (all levels, local to international) space.

The choice of spatial orientation of the program is one step in
forming a milieu. Spatial parameters for learning are defined, and the
level of program "cosmopolitanness" is chosen. Some programs,
for example, can be characterized as "classroom centered." Here
students and faculty spent most of their teaching and learning time
in one fixed point within the confines of the campus. Another
program can be considered social agency centered, because of its
orientation toward occupational and technical training and preparation for immediate employment for its students. Still another program can be orientated toward university and community issues and
development. Their energy flow would move out from the program
location into broader areas. A few programs might even have an
international orientation where teaching and learning takes place
in quite different cultural settings than that which characterizes
the campus. What locations are included and what locations are
excluded, for whatever explicit or implicit reasons, contributes to
the nature and quality of the social work milieu of a particular
program.

Undergraduate curriculum standards in social work encourage a
minimal definition of educational location that would include
campus, agency, and to a limited extent community locations. The
exciting and vital undergraduate social work programs would seem
to be those with considerable outreach, those that border on the
"university without walls" model. The search for new geographical
locations for learning requires special energy usually associated with
those programs that are most alive and growing qualitatively.

Many recent references have been made in social welfare circles to community-based programs and services (e.g., community-based corrections, community mental health). As in practice, so with education, there is a need for a community-based emphasis in our teaching and learning. Teaching exclusively within an "institutions" framework results in the same shortcomings as treating within an "institutions" setting. The ivory tower may once have been an exclusive repository of theoretical knowledge and educational resources, but today practitioners are better trained, and most are grounded in sound theory and participate in some form of knowledge testing and building. Practice agencies are repositories of educational resources and clinical experiences equal to many solid undergraduate programs. This changed reality must be acknowledged, and teaching and learning patterns must be reorganized to take advantage of it.

A strong community-based undergraduate social work educational orientation in no way implies any inherent weakness in our university-based resources. The classroom will continue to hold a prominent place in the higher education of the professions. However, educational milieu as a curriculum concept should lead us to think beyond the traditional boundaries of university-based education, and to include, in addition to teaching and learning, an added dimension—living.

A community-based educational milieu is one characterized by a constant movement of community persons (clients, practitioners, citizens) onto the campus and into the classroom. Concomitantly, it suggests the outflow of faculty and students into the agency and community world. The purpose in either instance remains the same—to increase and enrich professional growth and development process.

In many ways, the community-based orientation affords greater opportunity for faculty development at little or no cost to student development. The co-learning opportunities are greatly magnified, and the community base is a challenge to all. Operationalizing a community-based curriculum approach has been debated and developed in social work education over the years, and previous undergraduate social work education studies have given it considerable attention.[7] The educational milieu concept, and its component feature of "educational space," serves to reinforce this.

Practically speaking, the design of undergraduate education needs to involve both clients and practitioners in the design, delivery, and evaluation of instruction. Students and faculty need to make concurrent investments in learning (or teaching) and in community service. Such allocation of educational energies is absolutely necessary to free the educational centers from any charge of "educational imperialism." We cannot educate ourselves at the expense of the community, but only in ways that benefit the community (in both the long and short run). In subsequent sections, we deal with practical examples of how community persons can be related to the university program and how the faculty and students can engage in community work. Specific illustrations of how the community experience can be employed curricularly in undergraduate social work education are available through supporting references.[8]

Physical Place

Even where the geographical boundaries of teaching and learning are expanded, there is usually a program base point—a departmental home on the parent college campus. It is in this location that students register for their program; take some, if not most, of their courses; interact with each other and their faculty; and experience much of their formal education.

The physical form and arrangements of this base program location can be considered another component of educational milieu. Allport, in his excellent analysis of ego functioning, discussed one of the properties of the ego as "ego-extension,"[9] which he defines as the way in which a person extends him or herself through such tangibles as clothing, personal effects, etc.

Programs, as well as people, extend themselves through physical design. Most educational programs are located in assigned spaces that generally were designed and furnished for them. As is true in most institutional environments, the design of these spaces and their furnishings is based on efficiency, cost, safety, and maintenance considerations. Except where lab and classroom space are involved, consideration is rarely given to the educational impact of architectural quality, and within the educational program, few faculty or administrators think much about space and its educational impact, except insofar as their immediate comfort and convenience (such as the faculty office) is affected. We would argue that the physical-architectural features of an undergraduate social work program, if "modified" and "reshaped," can be creatively employed in achieving desired educational goals and objectives.

Physical space is like a blackboard upon which can be written important and vital educational concepts. All that is required is that someone take responsibility for writing on that blackboard—that "someone" being those who have a commitment to "what's worth knowing." We have suggested several possible educational orientations for undergraduate social work programs, such as human-caring concern, a cross-cultural orientation, or a multidisciplinary orientation. Fortunately, these kinds of goal statements easily lend themselves to an architectural or design translation, as the following examples illustrate.

The attempt to create a strong, humanistic, caring environment can be expressed through the way in which the educational system is "open" or "closed." There are all sorts of spatial symbols that are reflective of one or the other orientation. For example, faculty doors can remain open or closed; classrooms can be organized in a highly structured or a conveniently flexible arrangement; support personnel and administrators can be located for maximum accessibility to faculty and students or they can be isolated from routine traffic (so they can get their paperwork done). Office spaces can be furnished in standardized, government issue items, or they can be individualized and furnished by those who occupy them. A "space walk" through a typical program area will tell a lot about the educational milieu that is operating within that program.

It is common in educational institutions, particularly where classroom space is shared by several programs, to find classrooms empty and sterile (except for blackboard, lectern, and the inevitable hard chairs). What would it take to turn this same classroom into a center of educational stimuli? Would it be impossible for the occupants sharing the classroom space to work out a shared arrangement that would allow a wide range of concepts to be expressed within the interior design of the classroom, with, for example, paintings, photo essays, news clippings, wall murals, posters?

If the classroom can house visual and symbolic concepts, so also can hallways, waiting areas, and entries. Too often the educational corridor merely leads people in and out of the halls of learning, rather than to the halls of learning. One need only think of the hallway or corridor as an "educational mall" and the walls as the "gallery of education" to stimulate the creative possibilities of what is now wasted space. There is a need for more than announcements (usually of job openings or classes not meeting) and an occasional cartoon or poster in these areas. During a recent accreditation visit to one school of social work, visitors (including students) were greeted with a large billboard that contained a "provocative statement of the day"—a sort of philosophical thought twister. On the day of the visit, the sign read: "If social workers are paid to help others, why aren't clients paid to be helped?"

Having visited many undergraduate social work programs, one observation stands out—many are ethnocentric and class-bound. Few expand and extend ideas beyond what is already conventionally present in the local college-community environment. Even the programs in private colleges have an emptiness and sterility usually expected of a public office building. To educate our students and ourselves about cultural differences, to expand our awareness of needs and circumstances of special populations, to bring into focus the issues from around the world—these are some of the raw educational materials out of which the spatial design features of a program could be designed.

How much could a visitor to an undergraduate social work program learn about social work simply by walking through its environment? Is the social work program environment different from that of the history department or the math department? Could a new student, after a first visit, pick up a sense of the educational emphases of our undergraduate program without having to ask? Answering these questions would tell a lot about the status of a particular program environment.

The stated educational goals of the University of Iowa social work program cited earlier led to the design of the following physical features for its program environment.

1. Faculty offices were furnished by the faculty themselves with materials and artifacts of their own choosing, even sometimes purchased at their own expense. Each office, consequently, was highly individualized and personalized.
2. Some faculty, teaching assistants, and staff shared common work areas and/or were located conveniently near each other to maximize face-to-face communication.
3. Hallways were decorated with such displays as a photo essay on the family of man, posters of different ethnic-racial groups, and up to date news clippings on social policy matters.
4. Each classroom was decorated to express a different educational theme (international theme, alternative futures theme, family of man theme), and each was informally furnished with canvas chairs instead of standard classroom chairs to encourage open discussions and more casual relationships. Such chairs are "symbolic" of casualness and are easily moved to accomodate various levels of small group discussion.
5. Informal meeting places to accomodate extra classroom learning and discussion were provided: for example, a key area is a large, comfortable, student-run coffee shop next to the main classroom areas.
6. All furnishings were selected with a consideration of energy conservation and the need to recycle materials, as well as for their "softness" and comfort.
7. Books, periodicals, media tools, and even the computer were

physically located for their visibility and accessibility, to encourage use rather than to protect against possible abuse.
8. Colors, lighting, and furnishings were selected for variety, beauty, and originality.
9. Former hall locker spaces were converted into plant terrariums and built-in benches.

There is a growing field in environmental design psychology that affords a fresh theory about how behavior is influenced by physical environment.[10] Many social work clients are persons for whom physical setting is a strong determinant in the quality of life experienced. Conscious use of design of environment within a social work program can produce a "living-learning" potential and insure a pleasant environment in which teaching and learning can take place. People need symbols to live by. In the case of an educational program, the program's "symbols" are important for the program. The physical expression of these symbols should be created by the program to point up the program's educational goals. They can not be left to the parent institution. Shaping environment is highly satisfying, since the results are so apparent and measurable, and the educational goals of most programs are relatively easy to translate into environmental design features.

Human Social Network
Awareness of the potential of the physical environment to shape behavior may be somewhat new. Awareness of the importance of "significant others" to our behavior (even our program functioning), however, is of long standing. The mix and quality of the persons who share in the task of teaching and learning are readily acknowledged as powerful variables in defining the educational milieu. Faculty selection, student selection, involvement of other disciplines, and relationships with community practitioners and the client world are definitely crucial decisions that create the human chemistry of a particular education milieu.

We referred earlier to an analog—therapeutic milieu—and the attention it directed toward the role of the nonprofessional support personnel. This recognition serves as our first principle in implementing the human environment component. We would argue a position that *everyone* is part of the academic enterprise. There would be no one employed or connected to the undergraduate program who would not be producing or contributing to curriculum development-delivery. The milieu shapers (those with greatest influence on the educational environment) may be and often are persons other than the teaching faculty or the program director. Opinion leaders are present in educational settings and at all levels, and they frequently affect the students and what they learn. An exciting aspect of this concept is that it forces us to enlarge the field of "teaching and learning" by adding new people resources. It further allows us, in some instances, to identify some special curriculum opportunities that might not be available if curriculum were solely identified with academic teaching personnel alone.

We are familiar with an undergraduate and graduate social work program[11] whose *personnel* include two ex-offenders (faculty), a former AFDC recipient and a person on leave from a mental hospital (secretaries), a paraplegic and Vietnam refugee (CETA high school student aides), and a mentally retarded man (paid as "consultant" on developmental disabilities) who operates the school coffee shop. Each of these persons was hired because they could perform some assigned task while also sharing their special background and circumstances with others. Given the nature of social work, their special backgrounds had the potential to make a distinctive contribution in the curriculum. Each of these people, out of their own interest and concern, helped others stretch their understanding of the human condition and of the special needs and contributions those different people bring to an environment.

Assuming a program commitment to cultural diversity, the age, sex, ethnic, and racial composition of faculty, students, and staff become critically important to the educational milieu. A lack of "diversity" within the teaching-learner group necessarily handicaps an undergraduate program's preparation of professional helping persons who in their jobs must relate to all kinds of people.

Cultural diversity is a necessary, but not sufficient, condition for building a positive human milieu. There is a further need to insure equity in the roles and responsibilities of the different "representatives." If all faculty are white, even though there is a sizeable black student population, something is wrong. If all senior faculty are men, even though there is a representative number of women in teaching positions, there is a problem. Affirmative action can facilitate efforts to build a richly diverse human group, but a commitment to the concept of human diversity as an educational principal could make affirmative action pressure unnecessary.

A more questionable mix is the disciplinary background and experiences of faculty. Accreditation standards require that undergraduate social work programs have at least one full-time faculty member with an MSW. Beyond this requirement and a program's expected identification with the social work profession, the choice of who serves on the faculty is open. A commitment to an inter-disciplinary orientation defines a program's degree of openness and to some extent its commitment to a human services concept.

Faculty, student, and staff selection are all of equal (or at least near equal) importance when the concept of curriculum is broadened to the consideration that all personnel affect the educational milieu. People are the essence of social work. They are the life blood of educational milieu. Choosing the office receptionist can be as significant as choosing who is to fill a vacant faculty line.

Administrative Policy and Procedure[12]

The mix of people in an undergraduate social work program shapes the educational *milieu* of that program. The presence of people, however diverse their characteristics, may have less to do with milieu than the quality of their interactions. The quality of human interaction is obviously partly a function of who the people are (their personal attributes). Beyond this, however, the quality of human interaction (in an educational setting) appears to be influenced by administrative policies and practices of the program. We have therefore chosen to include the administrative function as yet another component of educational milieu.

The student in an undergraduate program experiences two roles: the role of learner and the role of student being administratively "processed" through the program requirements. The reasonableness and appropriateness of the administrative experience can become a significant part of the "media-message" interchange. The way a program is administered communicates to the student (and others) many things, including the philosophy, theory, and value orientation of social work administration as a practice method. Thus, social work administration can be at least partially taught through its own program administrative practices. For example, social work principles of self-determination and democratic participation can be demonstrated by the way students, faculty, and staff participate in educational decisionmaking. Shared (participatory) decisionmaking can be both taught and learned most easily through practicing and experiencing it.

Communication styles are likewise influenced by administrative practice. Programs in which everything must be "in writing " set a tone for human interactions—a legalistic and bureaucratic tone. Such programs necessarily become preoccupied with record keeping, policy elaboration, and the standardization of processing students. While formal, written communication is not inappropriate for undergraduate social work programs, as a profession we should be more concerned with humanizing bureaucratic procedures and building models of personal, face-to-face, individualized communication.

To communicate at a personal level, programs must be organized at a human scale and people made accessible to one another. The "note in the mailbox" method of communicating is too often a result of the fact that the person you need to communicate with is never around. There are schools where faculty show up for class, or an occasional meeting, and hold the minimum number of required office hours. By their absence, these faculty indicate they are either too busy or really not interested in students. Similarly, those faculty who "walk the extra mile" rarely go unnoticed and unappreciated by their students. In either case, the way faculty handle their administrative functions contributes to the educational milieu. A weak and deteriorating milieu is easily recognized by patterns of student-faculty avoidance and by a stress on secondary modes of communication.

Its policymaking pattern also suggests much about a program. There are programs that legislate a lot and make meeting graduation requirements an educational challenge in and of itself. These are the "educational bureaucracies." Other programs seem to legislate only in response to CSWE guidelines or directions. These are the "educational party liners." Then there are those that legislate only when necessary, to serve the student. These are the programs most likely to produce a strong, positive educational milieu. They view their program as being in the business of "individualizing" an educational experience; they operate on judgment rather than by rule and hold curriculum and related administrative legislation to a minimum.

One of the most powerful administration decisions is the allocation of resources (money, personnel, space). The flow of dollar-resource investments again tells much about a program. If an undergraduate program is part of a graduate school of social work and the resource allocation between the two program levels differs greatly, there is a good probability that a first and second class citizenship arrangement probably exists. But the amount of dollars available to a program affects its educational milieu much less than the way those dollars are allocated. How much of the educational dollar goes to administrative overhead? To faculty salaries? To curriculum resources? To the undergraduate program? To the graduate program? The answers to these questions help shape the "milieu" of a particular program.

Administrative decisions are central in the design of the human component of the program. Faculty, student, and staff selection are subject to administrative criteria and search-selection procedures. Accreditation standards influence these criteria and procedures, but most undergraduate programs work these out for themselves (usually within any policy-procedure of the parent institution). Actual experience with these policies and procedures introduces more "information" into the milieu. One can identify the attitudes and philosophy of a particular undergraduate program from its student selection policies and procedures. In our experience, there are a variety of latent (and manifest) factors and types that can operate here: the party liners, who simply meet CSWE standards; the conservatives, who attempt to screen out the misfits and to keep enrollment down (supposedly to keep quality up); the casuals, who avoid dealing with admissions selection since it's too much work; and finally, the milieu builders, who try to design administrative procedures and policies that afford optimum help to students in their career choices and intellectual growth. This oversimplification of admission approaches is not an attempt to create good guys and bad guys in the world of undergraduate education, but serves only to reinforce that admission procedures and policies go beyond admitting and selecting candidates. They add much to the "image" of a program and the milieu experienced by all participants.

The reward-recognition structure is yet another sensitive administrative policy and procedures area. In many ways, this is the most direct administrative tool for influencing the behavior of people within the program and the ways they will interact with each other. The criteria developed for performance evaluation—staff, student, or faculty—are critical; the way in which the performance evaluation procedures are carried out is equally important. There is also a process of "personal," as well as task-related evaluations that go on in a formal, task-centered environment. A marginal student, for example, could be positively recognized for personal attributes, even though he or she would not be highly regarded in terms of academic performance. The humanization of the administrative process is in part achieved through recognizing we are more than the formal label we carry in a formal organization. Our personal selves operate in an educational program as much as our student or teacher selves. Program administrators who respond to the person side of the enterprise have an added opportunity for reward and recognition, while the educational program becomes a dignified and supportive community. The payoff is of course great, as the "rewarded" and "supported" person in an educational setting is one who is highly motivated to do the best possible job, whatever it is.

In reality, the practice methods of social work occur and are employed (or neglected) in the day-to-day functioning of a program. The administrative practices in an educational program have the potential to become a core part of the curriculum, another instance of the reinforcing nature of the media and the message.

Role Modeling

If administrative practice within the undergraduate social work program can "model" social work knowledge, skills, and values, think how much more each person within the human social network can serve as a role model. Each person in the educational setting is in the role-modeling business, students and staff as well as faculty. Most persons, even those without a social work background, come to understand the basic ideas and the essential values of the profession, and most can tell whether what we teach is what we practice. The more our behavior reinforces the basic concepts and precepts of social work, the more our "theory" is validated to those around us. It would seem fair to argue that students should expect, as a way of testing the validity of social work ideas, that the social work faculty practice and carry out concepts and values.

Educational milieu receives a certain emotional quality from the of its participants. We would suggest that high or low morale among students and faculty, and even among staff, could be related to the extent that "practice" (local behavior) and theory are integrated in the educational experience. Students and faculty with low morale are generally cynical about their field. They sense the hypocrisy of the field. To these individuals social work is "academic," a nice thesis but impracticable. High morale is found among those whose behavior approximates the goals and ideals of the profession or those belonging to programs that collectively do rather well in these terms.

The expectation of role modeling can be unsettling, because of the pressures it places on a program. Fortunately, for us, our theory leads more to a "supportive" than a judgmental attitude toward those whose achievement is less than might be expected or desired. We need to be clear that the way students approach their student roles is part of the "curriculum." We should expect from them behavior consistent with social work theory and values. How students approach learning and carry out their roles establishes a pattern of behavior that more than likely will characterize their approach to professional practice. This is what makes positive modeling behavior in an educational setting vital.

We *become* what we *do*. Today's actions become tomorrow's expectations; yesterday's experience becomes today's source of energy. Undergraduate social work programs need to be able to say "social work is practiced here" as well as talked about. Together, students and faculty demonstrate how a program (of education) should be run, with respect for the dignity of the individual and concern for others practiced as principles of social work education, and with conscious and open efforts to serve as professional models for one another in the way they learn and prepare for professional life.

In this respect, there may be a need for undergraduate social work programs to strengthen their commitments to teaching, research, and service. Faculty who are deeply involved in community affairs, who express their professional views outside the classroom, and who actively participate and assume leadership in the profession more often than not will make a powerful contribution to a program's educational milieu. Too often undergraduate students have experienced a "flatness" in their academic experience, a lack of vitality, and an avoidance of the heavy issues. There is a hunger most felt in social work education. We need and want to fully express the intense "emotionality" of a profession that deals with human tragedy and human development. Scientific objectivity and rational thinking are important, but feelings, passions, and intense concerns deserve equal time. The best way to teach social work is to practice it. It moves us one step further toward building a positive educational milieu.

Melding Process

We have argued that educational space, physical space, human social networks, administrative policy, and procedure and role modeling are aspects of educational milieu. Of themselves, however, no one of these conceptional pieces determines milieu. Each are part of a larger gestalt.

A strong milieu (positive or negative) is one in which the components reinforce some central educational theme or themes. In a strong positive milieu, the orientations of the program are clear, and all aspects of the programs confirm this. A strong and positive milieu is one in which its orientations richly compliment social work knowledge and values.

Educational milieu can result either from indifference (a design by default) or from conscious planning and focused energy. Few strong, positive educational milieus happen by default. Most require substantial contributions by all persons in the educational environment.

It is our belief that educational milieu is needed as a concept in undergraduate social work programs. The apparent concern of many programs to meet minimal CSWE standards and, if accredited, to feel complete is unfortunate. Educational milieu is not a quantitative concept, it is an open-ended qualitative concept that should encourage each and every program to improve its professional performance beyond standards of accreditation and beyond the traditional view of curriculum.

NOTES

1. Thomas H. Walz, "Educational Milieu as Curriculum: The Administrative and Faculty Role" (Paper delivered at the Big Sky Conference, August 16-19, 1977).

2. Marshall McLuhan, *The Media is the Message* (New York: Random House, 1967).

3. Richard Almond, "Milieutherapie, Concepts and history," in *The Healing Community* (New York: Jason Aronson, 1974), pp. xxxix-xlii. Also, James K. Whittaker and Albert E. Treishman, *Children Away from Home—A Sourcebook of Residential Treatment* (Aldine Publishing Company, Chicago, 1972), p. 129.

4. Neil Postman and Charles Weingarten, *Teaching as a Subversive Activity* (New York: Delacort Press, 1969).

5. Reference here is made to our own social work program at the University of Iowa.

6. The author takes full responsibility for this conceptualization, its shortcomings as well as its strengths. Suggestions of other conceptualizations or other components would be welcomed.

7. *Undergraduate Social Work Education for Practice—A Report* (Washington D.C.: U.S. Government Printing Office, 1971), IB 15-9, vol. 1, sec. 3.

8. Thomas H. Walz, "The Community Experience in Undergraduate Social Work Education," in ibid., p. 71.

9. Gordon Willard Allport, *Becoming.* (New Haven: Yale University Press, 1955).

10. Thomas H. Walz, Georgianna Willebring, and Lane de Moll, "Environmental Design," *Journal of Education for Social Work*, January 1974, pp. 38-46.

11. Our reference is again to our own program at the University of Iowa.

12. Walz, "Educational Milieu as Curriculum."

Bureaucratic Functioning as a Social Work Skill

Robert Pruger

Almost all helping is mediated through complex organizations. For that reason, a welfare state *necessarily* is a highly bureaucratized one. Only in theory is it possible to have one condition without the other. Like it or not and ready or not, he who would be a helper must also be a bureaucrat.

Social work educators have never adequately come to terms with this unchangeable fact of the world. Committed to "welfare," they have enthusiastically tried to discover and teach the professional skills through which welfare is advanced. But, uneasy with or hostile to "bureaucracy," they have largely ignored the skills of bureaucratic or organizational practice that their students also need and that the advancement of welfare equally requires. As a result of this omission, social workers serve their agencies, their clients, and themselves less well than they otherwise could.

The implications of the above statement ought be clarified at all levels of training for the profession, since the first duty of all levels is to produce competent practitioners (including those who practice teaching and research) for service in bureaucratic organizations. The greatest opportunities, however, exist at the undergraduate level. Not only is the largest number of trainees found here, but the curriculum still has a relatively unsettled character. This paper makes the case for seizing these opportunities and, as a first step toward the needed curriculum improvements, suggests how they ought be used.

WHY TEACH "BUREAUCRATIC SKILLS?"

Every year, thousands of students are accredited as members of the social work profession. Armed with their college or university degrees, these graduates annually help refresh and restock the human service enterprise. The great majority leave school determined to help the clients assigned to their profession and typically believe themselves willing to pay heavy costs for the privilege of helping. But in a few years—perhaps fewer than the span of their formal training—their enthusiasm may be dissipated, their intent frustrated, and their professional efforts dulled. Many are jaded, alienated, and indifferent on the job, while what creative energies remain are spent elsewhere.

Why does this happen? Why are the promise of helping and the reality of not doing so so dissonant? One reason, as these young professionals soon discover, is that the helping skills they learned are less powerful than classroom and textbook discussions implied and their own preferences led them to believe. The knowledge base of social work, as some may now recall having been warned, is "soft." A second discovery is that the deficiencies and imperfections of service organizations can severely limit the amount of helping that actually occurs and that this would be so even if the practitioner himself possessed the most powerful of helping techniques.

But these two problems—an inadequate professional technology and poorly designed and equipped service delivery systems—at least are acknowledged to exist. No one denies that they are problems. As a result, the effort to minimize them can be broadly based and continuous. It would be quite difficult, for example, to find a single issue of a single professional journal that did not report some more or less promising advances in the knowledge that supports direct practice. Similarly, the random tinkering and the large scale formal experiments that make up the search for better ways to organize social service activities and to allocate social service resources go on endlessly, and at both the applied and theoretical levels. These days terms such as "coordination," "participation," and "decentralization" are as common in professional parlance as once was true only for such concepts as "ego," "neurosis," and "transference." With reference to these two problems, the best and the most social work educators can do is (1) expend the effort it takes to continuously update their courses with the new knowledge that does arise, and (2) help students better cope with the enduring uncertainties and imprecisions of their field, a field that must fundamentally remain an expression of art even as it more and more honors its obligation to try to be one of science.

There is also a third cause of professional ineffectiveness and demoralization, but this one is treated quite differently from the first two. To state the matter directly: *most social workers are unprepared for organizational life.* As a result, and by any appropriate criteria, they lose far more often than they have to. The existence of the problem is effectively denied through the simple device of paying almost no attention to it. The literature of the field and all school curricula strongly connote the belief that it is essential to train social workers in the casework and administrative skills involved in helping. But virtually nowhere does that vision include explicit instruction to increase the practitioner's ability to mitigate the stresses, avoid the traps, and develop the possibilities that inhere in the bureaucratic environment. The skill that comes with training is treated as being relevant to the solution of client problems, but the capacity to deal with organizational forces is left to arise from the student's untutored instinct and natural endowment.

The omission is, at best, surprising, since social work has always been an organizationally based profession. As implied in the endless supply of antibureaucratic anecdotes and jokes as well as in an almost equally numerous collection of serious works of fact and fiction, bureaucracy has a potent impact on all those it touches. With grand impartiality and equal facility, it seems forever to complicate the client's desire to receive help and the helper's desire to give it. The client's suffering is more regularly and perhaps more easily dramatized, but one instantly senses what Christine Maslach, University of California psychologist, means when she refers to bureaucratic "burnout." It is a newly coined term, but it refers to a very old occupational hazard faced by those who must take up organizational life in order to make their professional skills available to others.

Though all are vulnerable to bureaucratic burnout, any particular individual can do a great deal to strengthen himself or herself against it. Doing so is less a matter of personality or style and more a matter of mastering a relevant set of insights and skills. For example, simply understanding the enormous capacity bureaucratic systems have for continuing apathetic, alienated workers in office and on the payroll at least forewarns the individual to depend on himself or herself, and not on the system, if he or she is really concerned about not ending up as one of the burned out group. The organization offers the opportunity for salaried indifference, but it is the individual who must choose or refuse to go that route.

Obviously, a great deal more is required to avoid burnout than this single insight. One also needs to know, for example, what strategies and actions in what situations are likely to avoid this unhappy outcome. Such elementary insights are essential for a capacity to struggle better and longer and can (and should) be taught and learned at the outset of the student's career, rather than being left to the chance that they will mysteriously crystallize as a by-product of years of actual service-giving experience. It is difficult to see the justification or gain to anyone of leaving to a most uncertain natural process what is relevant to the practitioner's reality and can be explicitly taught.

Bureaucratic skills are as much needed to capitalize on the possibilities of organizational life as they are to neutralize its stresses and dangers. There is good reason to suspect, for example, that most social workers unwittingly either give up or leave underdeveloped the many opportunities to be self-directed that exist in complex organizations. Here bureaucratic skills can lead not only to greater private satisfaction with one's job, but also to higher levels of professional accomplishment and to organizational improvement or change. Insight is needed to recognize just what those opportunities are, and skills are needed to develop them.

The whole matter of bureaucratic skills would be of less consequence if there were any possibility of social work dissolving its historic ties to complex organizations, but that is not likely as there is no way to operate a modern welfare enterprise—especially one that already involves the expenditure as well over $150 billion of public funds annually—without bureaucracy. To be sure, some social workers, notably those who function as private therapists, can and do create entrepreneurial careers for themselves outside of the organizational arena, but the number who can do so will always be small, and the baccalaureate social work practitioner will continue to be the one least able to pursue this option. BSWs will go on shaping and being shaped by the bureaucratic environment in which they work. Clearly, the undergraduate curriculum should equip them to deal with this inevitability.

IDEOLOGICAL AND CONCEPTUAL BARRIERS

Several comprehensive barriers will have to be overcome if there is to be a sustained, effective effort to teach bureaucratic skills. One of these barriers arises from an ideological posture more or less adopted by all human service professions, including social work. This posture has two components. First, the professional service giver and the bureaucrat are defined by the social work practitioner as separate entities: you are one or the other. The professional calls, attends, and complains about staff meetings; evaluates, hires, and fires personnel; seeks to have his or her authority and resources enlarged, even if others must lose some of theirs in the process; and promulgates, obeys, bends, and protests rules. In brief, the professional does everything the bureaucrat does, but still resists any conception of himself or herself as a bureaucrat.

The second piece of ideological posturing explains why there is such a great reluctance to claim the title "bureaucrat." Here, not only are profession and professional held to be wholly separate entities from bureaucracy and bureaucrat, but they also are portrayed as being profoundly opposed to each other. By popular and self-definition, the professional is imbued with the virtues of knowledge, compassion, commitment, insight, and a high ethical code. The bureaucrat, on the other hand, is seen as being dedicated to the rules, rather than to humanity. Bureaucrats are attentive to higher authority, no matter how incompetent, rather than to science, no matter how well documented; they care more about the organizational budget than about the quality of the organizational product; to them, accountability means forms filled out in triplicate, but they know nothing of the accountability that is owed to common sense.

Many professionals trust the accuracy of these portraits. Furthermore, they believe that they are free to choose one identity over another. It should surprise no one that, as decent folk have always done, they opt for good over evil. Though the decision is ordinary and entirely predictable, many professional helpers experience it as a sitrring event and seize every opportunity to reexperience it.

Though this ideological barrer exists, it should be relatively easy to overcome in all save those hopelessly caught up in mindless visions of professional purity. For the great majority, it should be sufficiently sobering simply to realize the substantial harm that follows from a continuing refusal to take the bureaucratic milieu seriously. As many service givers eventually come to learn, they never were free to choose what they are or would like to be. Their professional qualifications may be what got them their jobs *in* organizations, but at least from that moment forward they are forever and inextricably *of* the organization. As mentioned above, they affect the organizational environment and they are affected by it. Unfortunately, most of this proceeds without their conscious, strategic involvement and in directions they would not have chosen. And *that* is the price they pay for confusing a superficial antibureaucracy ideological rhetoric for the complex body of insights and skills needed to manage a personally and socially productive organizational career.

Moreover, it is not only the professional who loses when she or he attempts to maintain an artifical purity. Some of the cost is visited on clients and some on the human service organization itself. Clients are helped less well and the organization becomes less capable as an instrument through which private and collective purposes can be achieved.

The second barrier is conceptual rather than ideological and will be more difficult to overcome. Though there is a great deal written about the organizational environment, very little knowledge exists that directly addresses the matter of bureaucratic skills. The literature of organizational theory is too abstract and is almost totally unconcerned with the practitioner's predicament. Theorists write primarily for other theorists, not for those on the firing line. In addition, such theory is written more to explain complex organization phenomena than to prescribe how one ought to behave under various bureaucratic circumstances.

Seasoned bureaucrats accumulate a rich organizational folklore, but it is too exclusively anecdotal. As a result, there often are substantial difficulties in distinguishing wisdom from wisecrack. Every social worker who has worked (or has been a student in) a bureaucracy has his collection of stories to tell, and many spend much of their time in the telling. The activity, however, is more cathartic than skill building.

The practical knowledge needed to deal effectively with bureaucratic phenomena will not spring up overnight—the penalty that must be paid for having ignored this dimension of practice for so long—and the bibliography at the end of this paper identifies some material over which faculty and students might profitably interact. And until appropriate case material is published, each school might attempt to accumulate its own. This is far from optimal, but it probably is the best that can be done at the moment. Though the literature is sparse, it is possible to specify some things about life in the organization that students should be helped to understand.

WHAT CAN BE TAUGHT?

A "Useful" Orientation to Bureaucracy

Undergraduate social work students probably bring to their professional education the same general suspicions about or hostility to bureaucracy that are pervasive throughout our culture. It would be unreasonable to expect otherwise, and it would be equally unreasonable to believe that their social work instructors do not at least sometimes curry favor with students by playing to this bias. (Unfortunately, there is some popularity to be gained in confirming the beliefs and world views students carry.)

Nevertheless, the many students who begin their organizational-professional careers armed only with the ability to ridicule or be antagonized by bureaucracy are as inadequately prepared as are those few who may leave school totally innocent on the subject. The innocent ones are fated to experience disappointments so severe that they can become disabled by them. They resign themselves to apathy and disaffection. The angry ones fare no better. They are most likely to discover that they are continuously betrayed by their own strong feelings. Spontaneous, emotion-driven actions or outbursts can have a dramatic, enduring impact in many situations (e.g., in family or other personal relationships), but this rarely occurs in the bureaucratic environment. It has too many ways to dissipate such effects, and the system easily exhausts and outlasts the individual.

The first contribution an undergraduate curriculum can make to helping to avoid these unhappy outcomes is to provide students with a more useful orientation to complex organizations than probably has been offered heretofore. The key word here is "useful." It implies that of all possible orientations, the one taught should be that which is judged most likely to help young professionals develop and maintain over time the most creative relationship possible to the bureaucratic environment in which they will spend all or almost all of their careers. Stating it this way does not directly identify what should be taught, but it does help clarify what should not be. It is difficult, for example, to imagine *any* test of usefulness that is met by a curriculum that leaves untouched or only reinforces either the organizational innocence or the great, almost automatic, irritation with bureaucracy that different students bring with them as they begin their formal professional training. Because both these polar orientations or postures are least likely to lead to greater effectiveness over time, they can be clearly rejected. The student needs and is entitled to better. A more useful orientation to bureaucracy includes consideration of the following elements:

Bureaucracy as the locus of social work activities. As indicated at the outset of this paper, society as a whole employs the bureaucratic form to achieve welfare purposes not because it is unmindful of what is wrong with it, but simply because there are no feasible, superior alternatives. For as far into the future as one can clearly see, the decision to pursue a career in social work will almost always also be a decision to spend one's career in complex organizations. Humanistically inspired preferences that social workers might have about the matter are entirely irrelevant.

Bureaucracy as both problem and solution for society.   As even the most cursory review of the organizational literature would reveal, bureaucracy has properties that make it singularly well suited to carry out very complex functions requiring the cooperative contributions of large numbers and varieties of specialized individuals. It has been said that other ways of organizing human effort cannot achieve even badly what bureaucracies achieve routinely. In this sense, bureaucracy is a solution. On the other hand, complex organizations are vulnerable to a variety of serious pathologies. Colloquial expressions such as "red tape" and formal expressions such as "the transmutation of means into ends" identify only two of the many well-documented and powerfully upsetting pathologies of the bureaucratic form. Nobody, including bureaucrats, wants these things to occur, but that does not seem to diminish their prevalence or virulence. In this sense, bureaucracy is a problem. Some have even referred to it as the major and most persistent social problem of our times.

The social worker as bureaucrat.   The individual social work practitioner relates to bureaucracy much less as some grand societal phenomenon and much more simply as an environment in which he works. The fundamental challenge for practitioners is to find ways to minimize the part that is solution as they go about pursuing their proper purposes in the system. Neither they nor anyone else can fairly hold the individual practitioner responsible for how the entire organization behaves, but each is fully accountable for how he or she individually behaves. And much popular myth to the contrary, the individual bureaucrat-professional does have very substantial discretionary power over his or her own actions in the organization. The fact that one can usually easily get one's colleagues to agree that this or that went wrong because of "bureaucracy" should not be confused with what careful analysis of any bureaucratic circumstance would reveal—that is, that every organizational outcome or event, good or bad, more or less occurs because some discretionary actors did this, even though they could also have done that. Even the fact that these actors felt that they had no choice cannot obscure the fact that some degree of choice always exists. No behavior, and certainly no individual, is a mere precipitate of the bureaucratic environment. Not only is bureaucracy not that powerful, but neither will any piece of social structure ever be so.

Thus, for those who must work in formal organizations, it is both unrealistic and unproductive to think of bureaucracy simply as a "bad" to be overcome. Rather, it ought be understood as a complex milieu within which private and collective purposes are pursued—purposes that are easily lost because the skills necessary for dealing with that complexity are often lacking. Neither the profession as a whole nor its individual practitioners can do away with bureaucracy, but they can increase their repertoire of skills for achieving their purpose through it.

Bureaucratic skill. Many would find the concept of "bureaucratic skill" a strange one. Skill, they would assert, is clearly needed to interview a client or conduct a meeting, but it is not nearly so important when it comes to negotiating the general and continuing problems of organizational life. By this view, what are needed here are not skills, but some desirable personal traits or styles. Thus, in order to win more often, individuals decide or are encouraged to be more or less agressive, direct or circumspect, tight-lipped or chatty, affable or reserved, openly one thing and covertly another, and so forth. The extreme of this view asserts that some personality types are ideally suited to bureaucracy and that others are antithetical to it.

Though many hold this view, they are incorrect. Personality and style, of course, have something to do with it, as they do in every sphere of social life and with regard to every kind of learning. But they are not decisive. Winning or losing is fundamentally a matter of the right behavior at the right time. No set of personal attributes ever has or ever will equip the individual to meet that standard, even with reference to the number of circumstances that arise in a single day. Conversely, there is no organizational situation that an individual is prevented from addressing skillfully because of his or her personality or style. Anyone can acquire the abilities and understandings bureaucratic life requires.

As indicated earlier, bureaucratic skill refers to the insights and abilities necessary to avoid the pitfalls, resolve the problems, and develop the possibilities that inhere in the bureaucratic environment. Because there has been so little discussion in the field about the entire matter of social worker *qua* bureaucrat, it is difficult to be much clearer here about just what this definition of bureaucratic skill really means. Hopefully, the rest of this paper, which successively and illustratively addresses the matters of (1) discretion, (2) organizational change, (3) problems of the long haul, and (4) ethical problems of bureaucratic practice, will suggest a useful meaning to the reader.

Discretion—How it is Lost, Preserved, and Enlarged

Bureaucracy does not *make* anyone do anything. Its power, which is awesome enough, is merely the power to elicit on average certain predictable responses to organizational situations. But each individual determines how close to or far from the average response his or her own behavior in any given situation will fall. Bureaucrats, in brief, are discretionary actors.

This entirely obvious point would not have to be made if students did not spend so much energy denying it to others and to themselves. And someone other than this writer will have to explain how so many bureaucrat-professionals can exercise their discretion even hundreds of times each work day, but still deeply experience their organizational lives as being devoid of freedom and choice. One suspects that the full explanation of this phenomenon has at least as much to do with the defects of people as it has to do with the defects of bureaucracy.

In any case, there are few things about organizational life that seem quite so important to help students understand as the scope of the opportunity that they, as bureaucrats, will have to be self-directed and still to remain honorable members of the collective enterprise. This is important for two reasons. First, there are many things about bureaucracy that tend to obscure the individual's awareness of both the degree to which he or she is self-governing and the even greater degree that she or he might be. Second, the most powerful defense individuals have against becoming, in the negative sense of it, "bureaucraticized," is their confident, carefully nurtured consciousness of how much they do and can create their own reality in the organization. Where this consciousness does not exist, there is no possibility of an individually felt accountability for what goes on in the system. Similarly, there can be no sense of how things might be improved by changing one's own behavior and strategy.

Putting it another way, the bureaucratic environment is, as it is reputed to be, like a stacked deck. But this means only that certain outcomes will occur simply so long as the human beings who staff the environment follow the path of least resistance. The social worker-bureaucrat who is satisfied with such outcomes need not be concerned with the matter of discretion. However, for those who are not satisfied—for those who hold visions, big or little, of what the organization or any of its parts *might* be—discretion is an indispensable, vital resource. Visions are empty and atrophy if never acted upon, but to act on them requires the appropriate degree of freedom to do so. Thus, as part of their professional training, students not only need to be helped to understand that they will be volitional actors in the bureaucracy, they also need specific instruction about how bureaucrats, through their own skilled or inept behavior, can lose, preserve, or enlarge the amount of discretion they have.

The question now becomes, of course, what would the content of that instruction be? How is discretion accumulated in bureaucracy? Unfortunately, the field, because it has historically ignored these matters, does not have even a vaguely systematic answer to this and the other important questions about bureaucratic skill. The classroom instructor who is willing to try to open his or her student's eyes to the possibilities must be prepared substantially to go it alone, at least over the near term.

The only help that can be offered here is illustrative. Consider, for example, a relatively minor bureaucratic event—the newly hired social worker-bureaucrat's first conference with his supervisor. In general, the new recruit loses discretion when she or he concedes to his or her supervisor more authority than is necessary. As a minimal condition, the recruit's professional training should have equipped him or her to make the appropriate distinction.

Even if nothing else is discussed early in the supervisory relationship, the content of newcomer's job will be. No single dialogue is quite as consequential. Commitments made here, even if only implicitly, quickly become settled items in the recruit's job routine. Once they become a part of the supervisor's expectations, they can be administratively enforced.

The supervisor will always have some conception of the job he or she wants the newcomer to perform. It may be extremely loose or very detailed. The specifications it contains may be derived from law, organizational rules, precedents established by one or more previous job holders, the supervisor's professional judgment and personal bias, or any of a variety of other sources. Finally, the supervisor will be more or less determined to enforce his or her conception of the recruit. Newcomers who want to determine as much of their own job content as possible have as their first task discovering all of this—that is, they must learn (1) the supervisor's concept of the job, (2) the kind and degree of authority behind each detail of that concept, and (3) the strength of the supervisor's intention to bring the recruit into compliance with one or more aspects of that concept.

Each of these three kinds of information has its own uses. Knowing what is clear and what is vague in the supervisor's mind helps the newcomer estimate where he or she might be able to set precedents. Understanding the grounding of the supervisor's conception helps in anticipating what kinds of arguments, if any, are relevant to each of the supervisor's instructions and therefore might produce changes in those instructions or, failing that, will at least be perceived as proper challenges. For example, whatever objections a newcomer might have to assigned duties that are derived from legal requirements, she or he probably will have no choice but to accept them or resign. Job components the supervisor justifies on the basis of professional expertise can be questioned on the basis of the recruit's own expertise. This can be done in the spirit of collegial dialogue and entirely without rancor, especially if one of the parties is determined to keep it on that level. Where the newcomer is being told to duplicate the behavior of a predecessor, he or she can probe to see if there is any deeper justification and, if unsatisfied by what he or she finds out, can ultimately insist on the right to find his or her own way.

Even if she or he loses this battle, the new worker will have communicated a message to the supervisor that should make a difference in the future. Finally, knowing how much the supervisor will insist on various details should help the newcomer better determine what it will take to win beyond merely having relevant or logical arguments. This includes the recruit's own tolerance for conflict. Lacking what may be necessary, a new employee may simply express his or her doubts, but reserve the struggle for a later time when his or her position will hopefully be stronger. In doing this, the newcomer will at least be consciously aware that she or he has deferred and why. Under these conditions, he or she is much more likely to equip himself or herself to return to the point, if it continues to be important.

The recruit can use these insights to make a bureaucratic career more self-directed. Much of this opportunity can be lost in beginning with the supervisor, however, if she or he fails to come to terms with the recruit's greatest vulnerability—the anxiety that arises out of the uncertainties inherent in his or her status and from which there probably is no immunity. Many of these uncertainties can be quickly resolved, but only at the expense of lost discretionary opportunities, and therein lies the danger. More than one supervisor has signaled the newcomer to "be creative," only to be met by a response from the latter that could be understood as, "Tell me what to do."

The urge for security, for the feeling that one is right on board, can be so great that recruits will often press supervisors to supply job specifications about which they are indifferent or that they have simply never anticipated. If the supervisor is willing and able to acknowledge indifference or lack of critical thought to the newcomer, the latter has lost little other than having revealed a readiness to be commanded. If, on the other hand, the supervisor is reluctant to confess this, she or he is likely to invent the requested details on the spot, and may even feel obliged to hold the recruit to them. In both cases, the recruit may enjoy an extra margin of psychic comfort from having more specifically authorized ways to spend job time, but this must be weighed against the discretionary opportunities he or she will later look for, only to discover that he or she gave them away soon after entering the organization.

Things other than the content of the recruit's job are likely to be discussed early in the supervisory relationship (e.g., organization and unit objectives, standard operating procedures). Here, too, there are opportunities for surrendering or gaining discretion. Indeed, the possibilities and dangers exist throughout the bureaucrat's tenure in the organization, even long after details of that first supervisory conference are forgotten. Thus, one can only hope that the field will get on with the task of clarifying for itself, so that it can then do so for students, just how it is that discretion in the bureaucracy is won and lost. Even awkward, unsure beginnings by classroom instructors working on their own would be better than implicitly or explicitly leaving unchallenged student belief either that there is no problem here or that bureaucracy is so powerful and evil that success is impossible.

Bureaucrats and organizational change

Organizational change is an attractive subject to many students and faculty. Consequently, it is likely to come up in classroom discussions even where the formal curriculum seems to allow no place for any consideration of bureaucratic phenomena. The problem here is that most treatments are not helpful. They are ideological in character, rather than oriented to skill building. In class, as in the literature, the matter is too often addressed as if the central problem of change is to convince people to be for it. Though it is difficult to identify anyone who has directly opposed change, somehow there is an endless supply of able advocates seeking opportunities to cross swords with this invisible enemy. The results of these efforts are as morally satisfying as they are intellectually dulling. Through them, audiences regularly experience an invigorating, personal commitment to change. Unfortunately, such vicarious experience is no substitute for the patient observation, hard-headed analyses, and consistent behavior required to effect real change.

Fundamentally, what students need from their professional training is some way to understand how rank and file social worker-bureaucrats can help shape the organizations that employ them. There is a great deal about both bureaucracies and the professions that disposes their memberships to resist or be insensitive to the need for change, but there are also many opportunities to instigate progress that are open only to those who work inside the system. Moreover, it is a game all insiders can play, regardless of their hierarchical standing. To be sure, those higher up in the organization are in a better position to press more directly for more comprehensive changes (and that is a major reason many do and should seek higher rank), but it is also true that no one is ever powerful enough to fully control the process. There are always unexploited and underexploited opportunities, for anyone wanting to help move an organization in one direction rather than another. Insights are needed that will help students recognize just what those opportunities are and where they can be found.

Here again, much of what potentially could be achieved through the undergraduate curriculum will have to wait for the appropriate content to be defined. In the meantime, classroom instructors, if they carefully analyze only their own experiences in formal organizations (such as the schools in which they teach), would come up with insights relevant to organizational change with which they could confidently begin the necessary dialogue with students. Among these should be at least the following two concepts.

Organizations—all organizations—change. Sometimes organizations change because they want to, but more basically, they do so because they cannot avoid it. For any given bureaucrat, the *kind* of changes he or she wants may not have occurred; or they may occur too slowly; or the individual may feel that she or he plays no part in the process; or for many reasons, the individual may be discouraged about it or oblivious to it. But none of this alters the fact that the forces and pressures that produce change are at play in organizations at least as powerfully and persistently as are those that promote stability. A crude but fair test of this proposition is the difficulty that anyone would have in identifying even a single organization that is today precisely as it was even a year or two ago. No such organization exists or ever will. The conventional wisdom on the subject, which implies that bureaucracy, unlike everything else in this world, has somehow immunized itself against change, is simply incorrect.

Organizational change is a continuous process rather than a sporadic event; everthing affects everything. Things are always happening that make it easier to press certain initiatives and harder to press others: a staff member quits, and so some clique or alliance is strengthened or weakened; the organization moves to another building with a different layout of office space, so the director casually observes one unit more often and another less often while heading for lunch each day; the budget is reduced, held the same, or enlarged, inducing some to throw up their hands in disgust and others to compete more aggressively for everything in sight; one kind of client problem appears less frequently and another more frequently. Each of these events upsets the equilibrium of the system to some degree, making it more internally fluid than it was before. The bureaucrat who is sensitive to these things and can think a few moves ahead is the one who is most likely to see that some greater or lesser nuance in the organization's evolution occurs because he or she willed it. Though change is the most continuous organizational process, the responsibility to bring it about is part of no individual job description. Nevertheless, the social worker-bureaucrat is as implicated in the phenomenon as anyone else, and there are participatory possibilities that are closed to all others, if professionals will train themselves to recognize them.

Some faculty members, because they believe they have not been successful in their own activities as agents of organizational change, will feel unqualified to lead students into an exploration of the matter. It might help here if they thought of change as something that comes neither in large chunks nor as a result of showdowns and other relatively rare and dramatic occurrences. Rather, it ought be conceived of as a never-ending, almost daily process of incremental manipulations and adjustments, each of which makes the succeeding ones more or less likely to occur and which, taken collectively, make the organization what it is. It does take skill to achieve grand victories that are visible to everyone, but few bureaucrats outside of those one meets in novels ever have such opportunities and none of them do so regularly or even often. Victory in bureaucracy is something that usually comes in small, quiet doses and is won through persistent, rather than flashy, action. The faculty member who can communicate the incremental rhythm of organizational change, illustrating how one creatively fits oneself into it, offers students a preview of the reality that, for better or worse, they will encounter as bureaucrats.

Even in the highly unlikely situation where failure has been total, the faculty member's own honest, intelligent analysis of what went wrong and why would be far more instructive than the glib, seductive reporting of wholly successful efforts. Indeed, instructors who can acknowledge to students what they might have done, but didn't, offer insights as good as those found anywhere else. At least students will be spared the superficial and ultimately destructive ideological descriptions of bureaucratic change phenomena that, unfortunately, so many are so ready to accept and repeat.

Problems of the Long Haul

One of the strongest indicators of the quality of anything is the degree to which it has met "the test of time." While this test is regularly applied in matters of art and esthetics, it is equally valid in judging the performance of bureaucrats. It is the most demanding test of all. The bureaucrat who lacks staying power—the ability to function creatively over the long haul—is least likely to be effective.

This is so because, as anyone can observe, things happen slowly in most complex organizations. Features of their design make this inevitable and to a large extent irreducible. Therefore, whatever ideas, changes, projects, or other professional aspirations the social worker may have, she or he will not be able to realize them unless she or he stays in the organization and keeps working for those goals over a sufficient period of time.

But it is not enough merely to survive as a physical presence. Inept bureaucrats do that as readily as skilled ones, perhaps even better. The real challenge is to survive while still maintaining one's vitality of action and independence of thought. While this challenge for creative living is faced by everyone, wherever they live and however they make a living, bureaucracy has a special capability, documented in countless works of fact and fiction, to pacify and reduce individuals over time. It tempts them to withhold the exercise of their creative powers, and eventually they atrophy. It is this second condition that makes it so difficult to meet the requirements of the long haul, and it identifies where so many long-term "survivors" in bureaucracy fail.

Any seasoned bureaucrat knows something that the nonbureaucrat can at best appreciate only vaguely—that is, that the slow pace of organizational processes frustrates, maddens, and defeats the bureaucrat-insider as readily as it does the citizen-outsider. There probably is no qualitative difference between the despair or anger felt by the needy client who has to wait so long to receive a service, by the crusading journalist who bitterly exposes the agency's ponderous delay-causing procedures, and by the concerned human service professional who has written several memoranda containing feasible suggestions for improvements but who even several weeks later is still waiting for a reply from the director (who, in turn, is impatiently waiting for some committee or task force to submit its recommendations about the problem). Moreover, the bureaucrat has experiences of this sort far more often than any outsider, simply because so much of his or her daily life takes place in the context of the organizational environment; and these experiences occur with reference to everything, from the most ordinary functions to the most complex initiatives for change.

Somehow the bureaucrat has to come to terms with the tortuous pace at which organizational processes move ahead. Two extreme adjustments are certainly incorrect: namely, that it is as bad for the bureaucrat to wholly accept the bureaucratic pulse as his or her own as it is to think, act, and feel as if that pulse did not exist or was irrelevant to his or her strategy or plans. The first extreme leads to much less doing than otherwise would occur, while the second can only result in a continuing accumulation of hurts that must sooner or later lead even the most creative bureaucrat-professional to throw in the towel. In this latter instance, the individual could easily convince himself or herself and even many others that the system was getting no better from him or her than it deserved. It would be at least as valid, however, to portray such an individual as just another of those well-motivated, decent professionals who simply did not know how to better meet the test of time faced by all bureaucrats.

One of the most valuable contributions undergraduate social work education programs can make is to equip students with the skills and insights that will help them to pass that test. Where professional training programs fail to do that, they increase the chances that their graduates will end up in the crowd of mere hangers-on, probably the largest sub-group of the bureaucracy's population.

The previous discussion about the ways and means of accumulating discretion is relevant here. With each consciously achieved increase in the discretionary content of one's job, the sense of being the subject rather than the object of action grows. There is no perfect defense against the erosions of time in the bureaucracy, but this sense of being actor, rather than acted upon, is probably the most sustaining one.

There is a very large number of tactics and understandings, large and small, that could help the bureaucrat struggle longer and better. No further attempt will be made to suggest them here. The present hope is merely that social work educators might come to agree that the problems of the long haul are a relevant focus of professional training efforts.

Ethical Problems of Bureaucratic Practice

Bureaucracy organizes the collective effort necessary to achieve social purposes. The work of the bureaucracy, however, is carried out by individuals who have purposes, wants, and interests of their own. Yet the code of ethics of the National Association of Social Workers substantially ignores the matter of moral burdens of the individual who is continuously faced with the competing claims of personal and collective life. The code well expresses the social worker's obligations to his or her clients and to his or her profession. But at least by omission, it implies that no obligations are owed to the organization that makes the social worker–client relationship possible (except in the negative sense that the worker is instructed to insure that the organization does not interfere with the rendering of professional service to clients). Stated otherwise, the code provides guides for the social worker *qua* social worker, but not for the social worker *qua* bureaucrat. Those who teach undergraduate social work students should do better by them here than has the professional association they one day will join.

The three vignettes that follow illustrate the many circumstances that can arise in which the social worker must make a moral decision between the competing claims of self and organization:

1. The social worker handles his or her minimum job responsibilities adequately enough, but also knows that he or she long ago gave up all the visions that he or she had for the agency. In addition, his or her relationships with colleagues have grown so stale or sour that even if he or she were willing to press one more initiative, he or she could not attract even one ally. Deep down she or he knows that the best thing for the agency would be to quit, making room for a new and livelier face to take over. But he or she also realizes that another job that paid so well would not be easy to find. The social worker enjoys the standard of living this job makes possible, and so does his or her family. What should she or he do?

2. A supervisor has one incompetent worker in his or her unit. She or he would like to fire the worker, but to do so would entail several hearings before appeals boards; preparation of a detailed, written statement of charges, and most probably, a rebuttal of counter-charges of having treated the worker unfairly. The supervisor has no doubt that the worker is incompetent, but knows that it often is difficult to prove that fact to the satisfaction of all those who will review the case, particularly the incompetent worker's lawyer. And even if she or he does win, it would take a great deal of his time to do so. While mulling the matter over, the supervisor learns of an opening in another service unit in the agency, a position in which the incompetent worker would be interested. All the supervisor has to do is write a brief, vague, mildly positive evaluation of the worker and the transfer would take place. She or he is strongly tempted to dash off the needed recommendation, but somehow it seems wrong to do so. What should she or he do?

3. The social worker believes that his or her agency is quite a good one. Nevertheless, it enunciates a policy to which she or he takes grave moral exception. The director explains why the policy was

taken, but the worker finds the explanation unacceptable and decides to resign in protest. A friendly journalist offers to publicize the fact, which would bring pressure to bear on the agency and might get it to rescind the offending policy. The publicity, however, would also strengthen the hand of others, inside and outside the agency, who have been looking for an excuse to launch a total attack against it. The friendly journalist calls and tells the social worker that if he or she wants to go ahead with the story, he or she must give the go ahead right now. What should the worker do?

There is, of course, no final or complete listing of all the specific circumstances that can arise in organizational life in which the social worker is called upon to weigh collective values against individual ones. Through the discussion of any sample of possible situations, the classroom instructor will at least convey to students the fact that life in the bureaucracy is not really so different from life outside of it. There is as much contradiction, complexity, and need for sound moral judgment here as there is any place else. It probably is as important to get that point across as it is to have worked out solutions to the specific ethical problems of bureaucratic practice.

CONCLUSION

The central point of this paper has been to argue that there is such a thing as "bureaucratic skill," that it is crucially relevant to a career in social work, and that students ought to get more help in acquiring it than they have in the past. With some good reason, the man in the street will forever go on complaining about bureaucracy. Social worker–bureaucrats should be able to do better than that.

BIBLIOGRAPHY

Bennis, W. "When to Resign." *Esquire*, June 1972.

Culbert, S. *The Organization Trap and How to Get Out of it*. New York: Basic Books, 1974.

Finch, W. "Social Workers Versus Bureaucracy." *Social Work*, 21, 5 (September 1976).

Green, A.D. "The Professional Social Worker in the Bureaucracy." *Social Service Review* XL, 1 (March 1966).

Hanlan, A. "Counteracting the Problems of Bureaucracy in Public Welfare." *Social Work* 12, 3 (July 1967).

Levy, G. "Acute Workers in a Welfare Bureaucracy." In D. Offenbacher and C. Poster, *Social Problems and Social Policy*. New York: Appleton-Century-Crofts, 1970.

Long, N. "Administrative Communication." In S. Mailick and E.H. Van Ness,

Concepts and Issues in Administrative Behavior. Englewood Cliffs, N.J.: Prentice-Hall, 1962.

Meltsner, A. "Bureaucratic Policy Analysts." *Policy Analysis* 1, 1 (Winter 1975).

Pawlak, E. "Organizational Tinkering." *Social Work* 21, 5 (September 1976).

Pruger, R. "The Good Bureaucrat." *Social Work* 18, 4 (July 1973).

Social Work in Governmental Agencies

Edward T. Weaver

Governmental organizations have become the major employer of social workers in recent years, in contrast to an earlier time, when voluntary agencies employed the majority of social workers. The impact of this changing "job market" on social work education is not well documented. While the trends in social work manpower utilization are generally known, there is too little evidence that social work education is attuned to the manpower needs of its major employer.

It is the purpose of this paper to identify factors and trends in social work practice in the governmental sector that have implications for future planning in social work education. The impact of practice in shaping social work education derives not only from the fact that government is the major employer but also from the increasing link between government policy and the evolving definition and parameters of social work activity.

Among the governmental agencies that employ social workers are those providing services to the mentally ill, the disabled, the aging, children, families, the economically disadvantaged, the socially maladjusted, the physically ill, and the socially and emotionally dependent. In addition, there has been an increasing trend evident in the employment of social workers as analysts in policy positions in both the executive and legislative branches of government.

The reference point for this paper is the public welfare agency, which typically includes services directed to many of the types of problems and categories of people noted above. As a minimum, the public welfare function includes income maintenance, including food stamps (for the economically disadvantaged); social services (for a broad range of social and rehabilitative purposes); Medicaid (health and remedial services for the poor); and other services to support employment job training and independent living.

Social work practice has been fundamentally affected by governmental action since the mid-1930s. Growth in the legal base and governmental programs during this period have helped to identify, clarify, and put boundaries around social welfare functions. The broader base of social work activity and clarification of functions has also been a major contributor to the call for a more adequate definition of social work education at several levels—bachelors, masters, and doctoral.

Social work education has been slower to integrate the reality of these changes. In some instances, earlier philosophies that were heavily influenced by the close affiliation of social work education with the voluntary sector seemed to hang on. The underlying idea seemed to be that voluntary agencies could provide all the services, and that government involvement was an intrusion, or at a minimum, a necessary evil which—if we try harder—could be temporary. There continues to be debate and realignment of services between governmental and voluntary agencies—not always without competition or open hostility.

Tracing the changing role of voluntary and governmental social welfare in the United States is relatively easy. Voluntary organizations created by the humane values of various groups of citizens— fraternal, religious, or ethnic—were almost the only social service providers prior to the Depression of the 1930s. That tragic time brought a new recognition and reluctant acceptance that some problems in the social sphere were so large and pervasive that voluntary action alone was insufficient. It was acknowledged by action of Congress and the president in the 1930s that government must commit itself—as an instrument of all citizens—to "promote the general welfare." From that time forward, a creative pluralism has been forged that recognizes the historic and continuing role of voluntary agencies in serving the needs of various groups of the disadvantaged. There has also been explicit acknowledgement that complex and pervasive problems affecting large numbers of widely dispersed citizens require a response by government.

The actual number of social service workers in government agencies is unknown. Including states, counties, cities, townships, school districts, and the numerous agencies within each, the number of organizations in the government employing professional social workers must exceed 6,000. There is no point at which personnel data for all these agencies comes together. However, using census data, Sheldon Siegel developed manpower projections for the Council on Social Work Education.[1] With fairly conservative projections, he anticipates increases in social service workers as presented in the table below:[2]

Total Employed Social Service Workers 1960, 1970, 1974, and Projections to 1980

Year	Social Service Workers
1960	95,000
1970	217,000
1974	300,000
1980	323,000–402,000

Based on past trends, it can be projected that at least 60 percent, and probably higher if only recent experience were used as a basis for this projection, of the increase will be in governmental agencies.

However, in recent years, a new phenomenon has developed that adds further shape and quality to the voluntary-governmental relationship. The emergence of government purchase of specified services for groups or individuals from voluntary agencies has occurred in large part since the early 1960s. While governmental agencies (frequently court systems) had a few scattered, relatively low volume purchase of payment programs prior to this time, the growth has been greatest in the last decade or so. Many refinements are needed in the methods and procedures in the purchase programs, and the roles of the voluntary and governmental agencies require further clarification. Nevertheless, this new dimension in creative pluralism in social welfare, if developed so as to strengthen both governmental and voluntary response to human need, is a positive force in social work practice, and one that requires careful attention in planning for social work education.

Future trends in social practice will be likely to see a refinement of the roles of the two sectors and a continuing increase in social work employment in the governmental sector. The prospect of welfare reform, with related manpower and employment programs and proposals for national health insurance, indicate that the need for social service workers in the governmental sector will continue and probably increase, and that the functions of governmental social workers are likely to be varied—one of the major challenges to social work education.

One final note on the current governmental agency environment.

A close relationship between professional social workers and governmental social welfare has developed in spite of the pursuit by both
education and practice of several theoretical affiliations and concepts
of practice. Even when each has failed to serve the other well, they
have been locked in the same harness—for better or worse. But
how—from the past and the current environment—can we create a
better understanding on which to build the future? Perhaps a better
understanding of the institution of social welfare as it operates in
governmental agencies and the role of social work in relation to that
institution is the place to start. Gilbert and Specht elaborate one
conceptual scheme for differentiating between social welfare and
social work while at the same time defining their interdependence.
In part,they describe the relationship as follows:

> The institution of social welfare is much older than the profession of
> social work. The institution serves as a mechanism for mutual support
> which expresses the collective responsibility of the community for helping
> its members. It consists of a series of programmatic arrangements for
> meeting needs through the allocation of income and services outside of
> other institutional channels, such as the family and the market. These
> programmatic arrangements are run by people from many professions,
> including public health, nursing, city planning, public administration,
> teaching, and social work. Among these professional groups, social work is
> most strongly identified with the institution of social welfare because it
> provides the greatest amount of manpower for the diverse areas of social
> welfare programming . . . the institution of social welfare is concerned
> both with rehabilitation of individuals who have personal problems and
> with the reform of society's need-meeting structures. In practice, social
> workers are engaged in both rehabilitation and reform activities.[3]

It may be useful for educators, professional social workers, and
agency administrators to seek a better understanding of the complex
and related responsibilities of the institution of social welfare, the
individual governmental agency, the individual professional social
worker, and the social work profession as the corporate or collective
body of professional social workers. For our purposes it is sufficient
to acknowledge that each of these entities is different, yet there is
often confusion of one for the other. One illustration of the confusion
is the frequent reference to the governmental agency as identical
with the institution of social welfare. The identifiable and visible
agency then takes the criticism that is due the less tangible and less
visible social welfare institution. Likewise, the individual professional
may confuse his or her responsibility for institutional change with
that of the profession in its collective role. Such confusion leads to

ambiguity of roles, responsibilities, and accountability among the professionals and the organizations within which they work. It is within this environment that we must look for the current issues in social work practice in governmental agencies and to their implications for planning in social work education.

CURRENT ISSUES IN PRACTICE AND
IMPLICATIONS FOR EDUCATION

All levels of social work education could benefit from an examination of current practice and its implications for social work manpower. This paper, however, will focus, to the extent possible, on implications for education at the baccalaureate level. It should be clear that there will be no attempt to sort out the relationships and division of role and function between the baccalaureate and masters level. That is a task that needs doing but it is not for this paper to propose such a hierarchy.

Examination of the contemporary governmental social work environment as reflected in what was earlier defined as "public welfare" will reveal a number of issues that should be taken into account in planning social work education at the baccalaureate level. From among many issues that can be identified, the following are significant for persons concerned with social work education at the baccalaureate level:

1. erosion of formal education as a criterion for employment;
2. changing models of service delivery;
3. government–voluntary sector partnership in service delivery;
4. growing need for manpower educated for flexible change in a dynamic field;
5. social workers in nondirect service jobs;
6. professionalism and the organizational work environment;
7. practice in the sunshine.

Following a brief discussion of these issues, the implications for education as viewed by the writer will be specified.

Erosion of Formal Education as a
Criterion for Employment
During the past decade, several significant events have occurred that have had an impact on manpower needs and utilization within governmental agencies. In many instances, public agencies, personnel specialists, civil service employees, and social work educators have

been caught short—change in governmental social service agency staffing has been reactive and unplanned. Governmental social service personnel report that there has been an erosion of personnel standards in many governmental agencies. These conditions are randomly reported, and it should be noted that no nationwide data exists to permit analysis of the extent of such declassification of social service positions. There is little doubt, however, that such actions have occurred in some jurisdictions.

Several factors may have contributed to the current uneasy situation, but the single change in recent years that caused the greatest problem was the mandate of federal law in the early 1970s to separate income maintenance from social services at all levels of operation. This action came on the heels of a major change that required that services to AFDC children and child welfare services (to other than AFDC children) be administered and delivered by the same personnel (these issues will be discussed separately later in this paper).

Other governmental agencies in which social work personnel are employed have experienced more evolutionary changes. There have been changes throughout social work in recognition of different education and skills related to functional task assignment. While similar changes have been experienced in voluntary agencies, the impact on governmental agencies has generally been greater. One recent influence—sometimes positive and sometimes not—was the major emphasis, started during the mid-1960s, to open up entrance to service positions based on experience rather than educational achievement. Programs such as New Careers (career ladder development to allow people to move up without educational or other barriers) and the utilization of case aides and paraprofessionals have had their impact on manpower utilization today.

Increased demands for personnel between 1955 and 1975 also contributed to the diversified, if not planned, use of a wider variety of experience and educational mixes. Having used paraprofessionals and B.A.-educated staff in positions for which MSWs were earlier sought, it is difficult to go back—in fact, frequently there seems no reason to go back. Many functions appear to be as effectively performed by less highly educated staff members as by more highly educated and experienced ones. To some degree, the difficulty may not be the displacement of MSWs by less educated and experienced employees. Rather, we may be suffering from the failure to innovate, renew, and revise the role of MSW staff members within a more sophisticated and changed agency, community, and professional structure.

Some have argued that the major, if not the only, rationale for governmental agencies changing manpower education requirements is financial. Simply stated, it costs less to employ people with less education and experience, and no doubt such observations have some validity. But even if the primary motivation were sound—to open up paraprofessional positions for minority candidates with less education—the secondary motivation may be less so if it continues to downgrade positions as a means of cutting costs even further. This is especially true when the justification for higher qualifications and standards is not founded on demonstrated differences in results. The burden of demonstrating the appropriate educational and other qualifications is on the administrators and social work program staff in governmental agencies, with help from social workers in the voluntary agencies and educators in the schools of social work.

Whatever the causes of downgrading positions—financial considerations, valid or invalid functional analysis, or shortage in certain types of manpower—the fact is that such changes are a reality, and the impact of such change is not limited to governmental agencies. There is a ripple effect in voluntary agencies and an immediate impact on social work education at all levels.

It is a compelling observation of the current scene that the lack of credible or accepted educational experience, performance, and workload standards contributes to inadequate staffing in many governmental social service agencies. Freezes in hiring and the almost impossible task of convincing a budget agency, governor, or a legislature that more or better qualified staff are needed result not only from inadequate revenues but from unclear and unconvincing arguments that more or better will make a definable difference.

It is appropriate to note that social work practice has fallen short of assuring adequate position specifications and classification. Insufficient attention has been given by practice agencies to differential job assignment that defines tasks, responsibilities, and skills with sufficient clarity to facilitate appropriate specification of position qualifications, including education. This issue clearly warrants action by social welfare administrators and civil service (merit system) personnel as well as by social work education.

Implications for Education.

1. Social work education should be prepared to increase the number of social work personnel in accordance with projected need. Analysis of where the increased need is occurring points to education for government agency employment and for increases in

both MSWs and BSWs, with proportionately greater emphasis on the latter. Projections by Sheldon Siegel indicate a continued increase in both categories.[4]

2. Social work educators, in cooperation with governmental agencies, should engage in the process of functional analysis of position requirements, workload measurement, establishment of performance standards, and the like, for it is in such activities that social work educators can become familiar with the needs of practice and can help in educating and interpreting to official bodies, such as civil service commissions, the requirements for professionally educated personnel.

3. Education at the BSW level should mesh with education at higher degree levels to assure an uninterrupted range of capabilities for the employing agencies. Continued improvements are needed in the BSW curriculum and in relationships between schools and practice to increase the credibility of the BSW in governmental agencies. As recently as 1971, the Council on Social Work Education criteria in the BSW requirements for accreditation included for the first time that one of the objectives is preparation for practice. If the BSW is to be a recognized entry level professional in governmental agencies, preparation for practice is the essential objective of BSW education.

4. Social work education must prepare the graduate with a mind set and skills to target activity toward definable results. This is essential to establish credibility of the professionally educated social worker. It is not sufficient to know more than the average person on the street—the professional social worker is accountable for *results*.

5. Social work education would do well to consider the formulation of Specht in his paper "Deprofessionalization of Social Work," in which he draws an interesting and, I believe, useful difference between social welfare and social work.[5] Social work education has perhaps concentrated too much on the latter at the expense of the former. Social work education of the future should take full account of the social welfare institutions, in which the majority of their graduates will be employed, when planning curriculum, field experience and course content.

Changing Models of Service Delivery

The way people are organized to deliver services will change over time. Education must take such change and the dynamics of the "service delivery system" into account. Illustrative of recent service delivery changes are:

1. separation of social service from income maintenance;
2. requirement for merger of AFDC and child welfare services;
3. increased practice specialization.

The federal mandate to separate social services from income maintenance was motivated by the expressed goal of moving the potential for using income maintenance coercively in requiring the client to "accept" social services. Social services, except in situations requiring protection, were to be at the request of the client.

Separation of social service from income maintenance was traumatic. Social workers had long carried both income maintenance and social service responsibility for a caseload. The trauma and lack of clarity in this arrangement were evidenced by the difficulty most agencies encountered in defining the tasks and functions to go with each part of the separated organization. Practicing social workers found great difficulty—in fact some would argue that the task is still incomplete—in defining and identifying the social service tasks. This speaks to the ambiguity of the social service functions.

Two additional delivery system changes required directly or indirectly by federal law and regulation further illustrate this issue. In recognition of the potential, if not actual, existence of inequity, the Congress required that social services to AFDC children (and families) and child welfare services be provided within each state and local agency by the same staff. In short, these could no longer be separate social service systems. Some decried the merger because it would so overload the child welfare system that no quality of service could be maintained. Indeed, many would say the fears have been borne out, but this is not the place for that debate.

At the same time that AFDC and child welfare were required to merge—a step that could be interpreted as a move toward a more noncategorical approach—there has been a strong move toward more categories of persons as the focus for service. The aging, the mentally retarded, the teenage parent, abused children, runaways, among others, have all been singled out for special attention. In many cases funding, service delivery, and accountability for each of these service categories are separate from other obviously related programs. The service system is untidy, if not dysfunctional. These changes in program and problem identification seem to argue for increased specialization in practice.

Implications For Education.

1. Social work education shares responsibility with practice for

identifying the social work tasks in income maintenance and social service. Curriculum should reflect such understanding and should focus on preparing the entering professional to differentiate between services provided at the request of the client and those prescribed by society to protect the client or community.

2. The specialist-generalist polarity should be recognized as obsolete. An approach to practice—through curriculum design—should be fashioned that leads to the education of what one person called "interchangeable specialists." The point is that practice and education have to deal with the demand for practitioners with knowledge and skill that are transportable across the categories, but who at the same time can "specialize" if the job assignment requires.

3. A more difficult mind set to overcome, but one that impinges on the effectiveness of professional social workers, is the unilateral attachment to "quality" service in an unlimited need and limited resources environment. Education, to the extent possible, should prepare for coping with high volume demand with limited re-sources—of money and time. Among other things, this has to do with the setting of priorities and the management of time.

4. Work management skills should be included in social work educa-tion to assure that the student can integrate the concept of theory and the application of theory in practice. Skills are required to facilitate time and workload management. Failure to learn such skills and to accept their essential nature leads to professional knowledge and skill being wasted because of poor workload and time management.

Government-Voluntary Sector Partnership
in Service Delivery

This issue was briefly discussed in the early part of this paper as one facet of the current governmental agency environment. Further mention is warranted because this emerging and growing service delivery alternative has long-term policy implications and certainly must be reflected in the education of social welfare workers who work in the plural system.

The types of issues raised by pluralism are illustrated by the two following examples. (1) How does the social worker in the govern-mental agency work with a voluntary agency providing service to clients of the governmental agency? Which agency is responsible and what are the limits of control and information exchange? (2) What should be known about a *balanced* governmental direct service and purchase from a voluntary agency system? How can knowledge about the effect of such policy affect decisionmaking in the present?

Implications for Education.

1. Social work education should place pluralism in a positive context. Balance between the two sectors should result in resources in both sectors being utilized to the best advantage of the person in need.
2. Knowledge about theory and practice in case management, interagency collaboration, accountability, contracting, and service and program evaluation are all essential for social workers graduated into a pluralistic service delivery system.
3. Social work education should be able to organize knowledge about policy options in this area to equip social workers and policymakers to make decisions that are focused on the mid- and long-term future. Shallow understanding of policy options and their implications tends to lead to short-term expedient decisions.
4. Education and practice must accept the delivery system as it is—plural. It is not an *either* governmental *or* voluntary option.

Growing Need for Manpower Educated for Flexible Change in a Dynamic Field

The greatest need in today's complex, fast-changing world is for flexible people. If there is anything that frustrates renewal of our helping systems it is people—including professional social workers—who are reluctant or afraid to change. Professional social workers should be flexible enough to do things differently, in new ways, to get results in a changing world. This should be obvious in a society that discards occupations and technology several times within the space of one person's work life. Social work practice, to be relevant, must embrace an attitude of flexibility and adaptability to new approaches to human problems.

Implications for Education.

1. Simply stated, it is the responsibility of education to prepare one to confront and incorporate growth and change as normal and essential to the maintenance of a viable helping role.
2. Practice and education jointly need to specify the work to be done—the results desired—and the type and qualifications of manpower required to do them.

3. Education and training systems must be sensitive to and flexible in adapting to changing manpower needs.
4. A dialogue with representatives of practice should be established and nurtured. It is essential for social work education, as for practice, that such dialogue and relationships deal with the substance of education and practice as they relate and serve one another and the clientele seeking help. The idea of faculty rotation back to practice, if it could be handled administratively, could be useful in keeping both education and practice in touch with the status of each. Something more than occasional consulting or part-time, limited responsibility moonlighting is required to achieve anything significant in this area.

Social Workers in Nondirect Service Jobs

A new development in the governmental sector during the last few years is the employment of social workers in legislative offices and committees and in the executive offices of governors, budget bureaus, and governmental commissions. While this appears to be new, there are many parallels in these assignments to the activities of early social reformers who saw the policymaking power of government as the primary means of bringing sweeping change. Today's social workers in policy positions outside of service delivery are having an influence on program and policy. Social work practice in government spans a wide range of work settings and uses of knowledge and skill.

Implications for Education.

1. The range of practice—from legislative and policy analyst to specialized social worker with a child abuse caseload—must be taken into account in designing a social work curriculum.
2. At the baccalaureate level, the range may be narrower, but at a minimum the curriculum should include course content "about" the full continuum.
3. At least an introduction to analytical and research methods could serve to prepare the baccalaureate social worker to understand and utilize research and policy studies as a foundation for practice.

Professionalism and the Organizational Work Environment[6]

There has been, and continues to be, a tension between the professional and the organizational work environment. The professional views his or her role as substantially self-directed, based on individual competence, and accountable to the client, the profession, and oneself. On the other hand, the organization (employer) has a mission and a responsibility to society by charter or by law. At issue is the understanding of the role of a professional as an employee of an organized and proceduralized institution of society's concern. It is in the context of this issue that the term "bureaucracy" is seen as the intruder into the "professional" freedoms and prerogatives of the employee. While such tension may be inevitable, it need not be dysfunctional if the role of the professional in the organized work context is understood.

Implications for Education.

1. Social work education must espouse a positive view of the organized governmental agency based social work practice. It is difficult to teach a view one does not hold.
2. Social work education should include content and practicum to prepare for functioning in complex organizations.
3. Curriculum should include content on the concepts and practice of professional and organizational accountability.

Practice In The Sunshine

Sunshine laws are spreading across the country, and in contrast there is increasing and heated debate about issues of privacy and confidentiality. The impact of legislation in both these areas is little understood. There is debate about a provider agency under contract to a governmental agency sharing client-related information. The debate is frequently around data required by the governmental agency for accountability purposes. Even more difficult is the handling of "treatment" information. There is an additional question about whether *gathering* information or *using* it improperly violates principles or laws regarding privacy and confidentiality.

The case record itself may be a problem. There is generally no definition of what a case record contains. What is the "official" record? What are the limits of social worker record keeping to jog their memory and are such notes part of the official agency record?

To what degree must agency staff meetings that discuss and make service plan decisions be open to clients or other persons? When is an open process dysfunctional? To these difficult questions there are no clear answers. But in practice today, the social worker will face the dilemma of these unanswered questions and must be able to move ahead to serve people as prudently as possible. Social work education cannot ignore these issues even though they often appear imponderable.

Implications for Education.

1. Social work education should include preparation for the "open" environment in which people must be served.
2. Practical information on privacy and confidentiality issues should be included as well as preparation for appropriate sharing of information as required within a complex helping system.
3. In its role of expansion of the knowledge base, social work education should explore, research, and experiment with new approaches to balancing the "need to know" of professionals with the right to privacy of clients.

FOCUS ON THE FUTURE

There is a reciprocal responsibility of social work practice and education to design and execute an educational program that will enable practice to respond to human need with professionally educated personnel. Hollis and Taylor describe the essential nature and interdependence of practice and education as follows:

> Education for social work. . . grew out of the needs and efforts of practitioners and retains its vitality by remaining close to practice. Any attempt to evaluate the major developments in education should, therefore, take into consideration the relationship of education to developments in the field of practice. Neither education nor practice can be seen with any degree of validity without reference to the other.[7]

Two way influence is essential and deliberate, and conscious actions must be taken to assure that social work education is responsive to the needs of practice. It is moot as to which partner—practice or education—leads to knowledge of effective and workable interventive strategies with individuals or groups of people in need. Representatives of practice are obligated to work with social work educators to assure that the manpower needs of practice are met and to cooperate in the extension of knowledge through the scholarly study and research that is an appropriate function of the academic community. Arnulf Pins' "Changes in Social Work Education and Their Implications for Practice" captures the importance of this cooperative endeavor: "Social work practice has an important stake and role in what happens in social work education in the years ahead. Social work education, in order to continue to change and improve, requires more frequent, consistent input from social work practitioners and agency executives and boards."[8]

Practice and education can reinforce each other's effectiveness through ongoing collaboration. Conceptual foundations and organized knowledge, the tools of the educator, are not developed in a vacuum. Rather, it is the examination of practice and the input of practitioners with new ideas and methods that makes possible the refinement of the knowledge base and the skills essential to serving people in need.

The above perspectives are true for all levels of social work education, but are perhaps particularly important in the emergence and refinement of the BSW as the entrance level to professional practice. Clearly, professional education for social work practice at the BSW level is here to stay and is growing in use. The BSW credentials should be increasingly recognized by manpower and personnel planners in governmental agencies. The continued growth in numbers of BSW graduates and job holders should lead to the additional salutory benefit of an examination of the other levels of social work education.

If a single conclusion or implication for social work practice and education emerges from this paper, it should be that social work education has its continued existence in and for social work practice—much of which is in governmental agencies. Therefore, the two, practice and education, must confront the future together. The problems each faces in preparing and utilizing social service professionals can best be resolved that way—together.

NOTES

1. Sheldon Siegal, *Social Service Manpower Needs: An Overview to 1980* (New York: Council on Social Work Education, 1975).
2. Ibid., pp. 7, 16.
3. Neil Gilbert and Harry Specht, *The Emergence of Social Welfare and Social Work* (Itasca, Ill.: F.E. Peacock Publishers, 1976), pp. 3-5.
4. Siegel, p. 16.
5. In Gilbert and Specht, pp. 500-501.
6. The paper by Robert Pruger written for this project (see above) is an excellent and more exhaustive discussion of this issue.
7. Ernest Hollis and Alice L. Taylor, *Social Work Education in the United States* (New York: Columbia University Press, 1951), p. 3.
8. In Gilbert and Specht, p. 429.

Appendix B

Knowledge, Values, and Skills Essential for the Attainment of the Entry Level Competencies; A Complete Elaboration

COMPETENCY 1

Identify and assess situations where the relationship between people and social institutions needs to be initiated, enhanced, restored, protected, or terminated.

Fundamental Skills

1. Utilizing one's own professional self—skill in maintaining a frame of reference based on professional ethics throughout the assessment process; skill in recognizing aspects of one's own behavior that affect interviewing and relationship development and in controlling and/or using these behaviors in a purposeful way.
2. Responding to human diversity—skill in recognizing, respecting, and accepting differences in needs, communication and relationship styles, and personal and group goals as manifested by diverse cultural and lifestyle groups; recognizing how these differences affect the experiences that these groups have with the social institutions of the dominant society.
3. Identifying social problems—skill in utilizing personal experience as well as professional literature and the mass media to be aware of social problems at the societal and community levels.
4. Involving client populations in practice activities—skill in educating client systems about the need for and process of assessment; encouraging client systems to share their beliefs and

perceptions about situations and needs; making special efforts to help involuntary client systems participate in assessment activities to the maximum extent possible.

5. Relating to others—skill in relating to others with warmth, respect, and professionalism; creating an open, accepting atmosphere in relationships with others that encourages communication and sharing of affect and information.

6. Observing activities and situations—skill in observing conditions within which activities occur; relating conditions to activities; observing behaviors; relating observations to verbal statements; interpreting behaviors and situations.

7. Interviewing—skill in communicating with others in a purposeful way so as to exchange information needed for assessment activities; communicating effectively in bicultural situations; communicating effectively in bilingual situations (as appropriate).

8. Recording—skill in keeping records of interviews, observations, and other pertinent activities and interactions that are accurate and sufficient for assessment purposes, and that are within legal definitions of confidentiality.

9. Collecting data—skill in the use of research techniques and printed sources to obtain information about the functioning of social institutions; about unmet individual, community, and societal needs; and about problems in interactions between people and social institutions.

10. Analyzing policy—skill in identifying institutional policies and activities; describing the impact these have on client systems.

11. Using collegial networks—skill in communicating-interacting with colleagues to share and/or clarify information pertinent to assessment activities.

12. Using family, group, community networks—skill in communicating-interacting with relevant persons and groups to obtain and/or clarify information pertinent to assessment activities.

13. Interpreting and assessing—skill in relating pieces of information to define patterns of behavior; identifying existing or potential problems in the relationship between people and social institutions on the basis of information obtained; relating identified problems to existing or needed social welfare services or service delivery strategies.

Conceptual Knowledge

1. Culture—knowledge of culture as a concept; culture as a foundation for organized human existence; subcultures; the interface of cultures and of subcultures.

a. Cultural relativity—knowledge of the diversity that character-izes the ways different cultural, racial, ethnic, and lifestyle groups effectively organize to meet similar needs; major cul-tural, racial, ethnic, and lifestyle groups in the U.S.

b. Cultural transitions—knowledge of the migration patterns of different cultural groups; stages of cultural change during pe-iods of adjustment to new environments and situations; changing needs and changing resources of cultural groups at different stages in the migration and adjustment experiences.

2. Values—knowledge of values as a concept; potential for value conflict.

a. Cultural values and their impact on social organization—knowledge of major American values (and value inconsisten-cies); processes by which values get translated into behavior (norms, roles, institutions); strategies for resolving value conflicts.

b. Group values and behavior patterns—knowledge of major values of different cultural, racial, ethnic, and lifestyle groups; ways these values affect behavior; potential areas of conflict and/or misinterpretation between different groups and between them and societal values; different objectives-priorities between groups.

c. Professional ethics—knowledge of professional ethics; use of accountability to user groups as part of professional self-evaluation and evaluation of services-resources.

d. Personal values and ethics—knowledge of one's own values; ethical behaviors to operationalize one's own values; sources of conflict between one's own values and those of other in-dividuals, groups, or organizations.

3. Social problems—knowledge of the concept of social problems; major ways of defining social problems; distinguishing between a social problem and a personal trouble.

a. Describing and defining social problems—knowledge of the incidence, characteristics, and severity of social problems; reasons why potentially problematic behavior may not be defined as a social problem.

b. Major social problems—knowledge of institutionally created and maintained social problems, such as racism, sexism, and poverty; the relationship of economic exploitation and politi-cal disenfranchisement to the creation and maintenance of social problems and majority-minority groups.

c. Effects of social problems—knowledge of impact of social problems and of society's responses to them on people's lives, including the creation of personal unhappiness, conflict, and maladjustment as well as intergroup conflicts, competition, and powerlessness; impact of other behaviors not defined as social problems on people's lives.

d. Social problems and social welfare services-resources—knowledge of the social welfare services-resources provided to help people solve social problems; areas of unmet needs; sources of resistance to developing effective social welfare services-resources for certain problematic conditions and/or for certain client populations.

4. Social institutions—knowledge of the concept of social institution; realtionship between concepts of culture, social organization, and social institution.

a. Major social institutions (the family, education, religion, politics, and economics)—knowledge of the major social institutions; the manifest and latent functions of each of the major institutions; the social structure of each of the major institutions; relationships between institutions; the impact of each institution on the creation or resolution of social problems; the relationship between each institution and the social welfare institution.

b. The social welfare institution—knowledge of the functions and social structure of the social welfare institution as they have developed over time; social work roles in the social welfare institution; the mediating function of social welfare in relationship to the other social institutions.

c. Social work as a profession—knowledge of the historical development of social work; the relationship of social work to other helping professions; the structure of the profession of social work; peer review as part of professional activity.

5. Social system—knowledge of the concept of social system; homeostasis and system functioning; system boundaries and interactions with other systems; social institutions as social systems.

a. The structure of resource and delivery systems—knowledge of the structure of social welfare programs (categories of needs met for which populations, and types of agencies responsible for administering-delivering categories of service); knowledge of informal and indigenous helping networks.

b. Service gaps and biases—knowledge of the gaps in services existing in the structure of social welfare programs; service delivery problems; special problems faced by members of diverse groups.

c. Comparative social welfare systems—knowledge of approaches to need identification and service delivery used in other societies; strengths and weaknesses of alternative approaches; use of formal and informal helping networks; relationship of social welfare structures to societal objectives and structures.

6. Community—knowledge of the concept of community; geographical and common interest communities; communities as systems; the social organization of communities; community typologies.

   a. Group responses to need in a community—knowledge of the responses to types of need by diverse groups in a community; helping networks existing among diverse groups; compatibility of indigenous (natural) and societal helping networks-systems; obstacles to using societal social welfare services-resources in a community.

   b. Community change—knowledge of migratory patterns in American society; processes of adjustment when moving from rural to urban communities; dynamics of group interaction between groups when new groups move into a community; immediate and long-term changes within groups when they experience migration.

7. Communication—knowledge of communication media; the process of communication (encoding, transmission, decoding); the medium as the message.

   a. Form of communication and clarity of transmission—knowledge of factors affecting form of transmission; factors affecting interpretation when received; organizational coding and interaction with values of diverse groups; organizational impersonality and ability to reach subjectively oriented individuals-groups.

   b. Communication within and between groups—knowledge of formal and informal communication patterns within formally and informally structured groups; knowledge of potential communication channels between groups, including between formal and informal groups; communication patterns between groups with different values, norms, and expectations; communication patterns between groups with different types and amounts of power.

   c. Purposes of communication—knowledge of the different reasons for communications; effect of purpose on nature of the communication (roles of participants, objectives sought, conditions needed for effective communication).

   d. Interviewing—knowledge of the interviewing process as used in social work; dynamic interaction of the phases of interviewing; types of involvement by social workers, clients, and others in the interviewing process.

    e. Nonverbal communication—knowledge of the significance of nonverbal communication; observational techniques; strategies for controlling-using one's own nonverbal communication.

    f. Recording—knowledge of reasons for preserving communication; recording as an obstacle to communication; techniques for recording (manual and electronic) and appropriate uses of them.

8. Interpersonal influence—knowledge of the concept of individual change through social influences; sources of interpersonal influence.

    a. Relationship—knowledge of the use of referent power to create an atmosphere of mutuality, trust, and respect; the use of modeling to facilitate communication and exchange; self-awareness in facilitating the demonstration of empathy and the purposeful use of self.

9. Social change—knowledge of the concept of social change; factors facilitating change; obstacles to change; social planning and social policy as sources and processes of change.

    a. Problem-solving process—knowledge of techniques to identify problems; techniques for assessing resources to solve problems; techniques for mobilizing resources; techniques for evaluating problem-solving efforts; techniques for using assessment to formulate and/or clarify goals for the intervention effort.

    b. Policy analysis—knowledge of policies affecting the functioning of social institutions; strategies for identifying policy gaps, inadequacies, inequities.

10. Research—knowledge of methods of systematic problem formulation, data collection, and data analysis.

    a. Problem formulation—knowledge of existing information (empirical and conceptual) on which one needs to build; formulating relationships between variables so that they can be tested.

    b. Information gathering—knowledge of methods of effective information gathering in informal interaction; methods useable in situations primarily structured for another purpose; methods useable with members of diverse groups; use of automated information and referral systems.

    c. Data collection—knowledge of methods of data collection using formal data collection techniques; use of printed sources of existing data.

d. Data analysis—knowledge of methods of data analysis useable with subjective and unstructured information; methods of data analysis with small and large amounts of data; appropriate uses of statistical tests and computerized data analysis.

e. Organization of results—knowledge of methods to organize the results of data anlysis to assess the impact of helping systems on people who use them.

f. Evaluative research—knowledge of social indicators; research methodologies to evaluate program effectiveness; strategies for identifying relevant variables.

g. Ethics of research with human subjects—knowledge of the ethical issues involved in research with human subjects; strategies for maintaining confidentiality; procedures to appropriately involve human subjects in research planning, schedules, and procedures; strategies to avoid unnecessary interference in subjects' lives; strategies for recognizing and dealing with resistance by subjects.

COMPETENCY 2

Develop and implement a plan for improving the well-being of people based on problem assessment and exploration of obtainable goals and available options.

Fundamental Skills

1. Using professional ethics—skill in using professional ethics as a filter through which planning ideas and implementation strategies are evaluated.

2. Involving client populations in practice activities—skill in encouraging the client system to express preferences and to identify natural resource networks for use in plan implementation; planning so that members of the client system have clearly defined roles in plan implementation; planning for involuntary clients when necessary, but always trying to be sensitive to their needs and preferences and to involve them as much as possible.

3. Involving community persons in practice activities—skill in identifying community persons, groups, and organizations that could be useful in planning and plan implementation; involving community persons, groups, and organizations in planning activities as appropriate; utilizing already existing community resources; identifying specific roles in plan implementation for community persons, groups, organizations, as appropriate.

4. Evaluating resources—skill in identifying potential resources;

evaluating the probable costs and effects of using potential resources; evaluating the suitability of potential resources for diverse groups that will be affected by the plan.

5. Using human diversity as a component of practice—skill in recognizing the strengths of individuals and groups; building natural helping systems into planning; recognizing the continuum of human diversity when formulating and assigning intervention activities.

6. Identifying goals—skill in using problem assessment, resource evaluation, and client-community input to identifying feasible intervention goals.

7. Selecting appropriate intervention strategies—skill in selecting intervention strategies appropriate to worker, client, community, resources; selecting intervention strategies that are likely to be successful in achieving the identified goals.

8. Contracting—skill in reaching agreement with the client system as to the intervention plan, including objectives, strategies, worker and client roles, and evaluation procedures.

9. Facilitating interpersonal activities—skill in relating to others singly and in groups; helping those involved in the intervention effort to relate to each other, and to facilitate each other's work; solving interpersonal hostilities when possible and appropriate and clarifying misunderstandings; using oneself in a purposeful way to facilitate the attainment of the intervention objectives.

10. Mobilizing—skill in activating resources by assisting people engaged in plan implementation; maintaining momentum within the contacted time frame for goal(s) achievement.

11. Supporting and encouraging—skill in stimulating confidence among those engaged in plan implementation; providing support at times of discouragement or fear.

12. Functioning effectively in organizations—skill in functioning within formal organizations so as to use them appropriately to help achieve intervention objectives.

13. Using policy effectively—skill in working within the limits of existing policy but using every available resource including policy change as an intervention goal as appropriate.

Conceptual Knowledge

1. Values (see Competency 1 for this concept and subsections a-c)
   a. Cultural values and their impact in social organization
   b. Group values and behavior patterns

c. Professional ethics
2. Community (see Competency 1 for this concept and subsection a)
   a. Group responses to need
   b. Community influence and power structures—knowledge of types of communities; common power bases in different types of communities; sources of access to community influentials.
3. Social systems (see Competency 1 for this concept and subsections a and b)
   a. The structure of resource and delivery systems
   b. Service gaps and biases
   c. Resource information—knowledge about helpful sources of information when seeking to identify resources, services and opportunities.
4. Interpersonal influence (see Competency 1, subsection 8, for this concept, and subsection 8a).
   a. Relationship
   b. Group communication and decisionmaking—knowledge of patterns of group communication; types of group decision-making processes; leadership roles; group goals and decision-making strategies; group influences on individual behaviors.
   c. Situationally specific social work intervention strategies—knowledge of interventive strategies possible and appropriate in specific practice situations.
   d. Intervention roles and activities—knowledge of the professional, client system, and resource system roles and activities appropriate for specific intervention strategies.
   e. Practice literature—knowledge of major sources of information; major findings in the practice literature about the effects of intervention strategies commonly used by baccalaureate level social workers.
   f. Reinforcement—knowledge of the use of positive reinforcement to encourage and support activities.
5. Social change (see Competency 1, subsection 9, for this concept, and subsections 9a and b).
   a. Problem-solving process
   b. Policy analysis
   c. Social planning process—knowledge of functions of social planning; strategies for identifying persons and resources to use in the planning process; techniques to identify parameters within which planning must occur; strategies for facilitating planning efforts; linkages between planning, policy, and implementation.
   d. Policy formation—knowledge of levels of policy formation (governmental, community, organizational); strategies to identify

areas in which policy is needed (new or modified); techniques for clarifying objectives; strategies to clarify policymaking structures and procedures; strategies for facilitating policy efforts.

e. Networks of social agencies—knowledge of structures for agency input into community planning; systematic interchange between social agencies and community structures; professional roles in community planning; strategies for involving client systems in community planning; accountability, evaluation, and planning; teamwork strategies with colleagues.

f. Networks of professional organizations—knowledge of the involvement of professional organizations in community planning and policymaking and strategies to initiate or increase their involvement.

g. Citizen participation in program implementation—knowledge of strategies to inform citizens of program-planning and policy activities; strategies to identify roles for professionals and citizens in program implementation; strategies for providing support and technical assistance for citizens as needed in program implementation activities; strategies for the involvement of involuntary clients.

h. Self-help as a helping approach—knowledge of values supporting self-help; relationship of self-help to structured helping programs; self-help and the need for resources.

i. Contracting—knowledge of the purposes of contracting; the persons-groups that need to be included in the contracting process; strategies for developing a feasible timetable and appropriate evaluation criteria; procedures for developing and assigning activities-roles.

j. Reinforcement—knowledge of the use of positive reinforcement to encourage and support activities.

6. Formal organizations—knowledge of the concept of formal organization; formal and informal structures in formal organizations; formal organizations and bureaucracies; characteristics of bureaucratic functioning; alternatives to formal organizations.

a. Organizational procedures affecting formal and informal access mechanisms—knowledge of the procedures organizations use to control access to its services-resources; values underlying these procedures; impact of these procedures on categories of users.

b. Principles of organizational functioning—knowledge of the major components of organizational structures; organizational decisionmaking processes; organizational goals and effects on structure; organizational pathologies; organizational obstacles to service delivery; issues of accountability.

c. Organizations as systems—knowledge of the internal dynamics of organizational functioning; permeability of organizational boundaries and exchange of resources; impact of organizations on external systems.
d. Organizational goals—knowledge of coercive, utilitarian, and shared interest organizations and their effect on goals and interaction; professional roles in different types of organizations; compatibility of professional ethics with objectives and structure of different types of organizations.
e. Interaction and communication patterns in organizations— knowledge of formal and informal relationships; personal relationships and motivation in formal organizations; functions and dysfunctions of formal communication patterns; alternative uses of communication channels; problems of access by outsiders, including consumers; internal motivation and service quality; humanizing formal structures to deal with personal problems and affect.
f. Power relations in organizations—knowledge of formally allocated power; personal sources of power; organizational power and its effects on consumers; organizational power and countervailing power relationships.
g. Principles of teamwork—knowledge of appropriate roles of persons in organizations; potential for cooperation with persons in other organizations; need to respect the prerogatives and limits of one's own and other's positions; ways of clarifying role conflicts; strategies to reduce competition.
h. Practice objectives and service structures—knowledge of issues in organizing to meet practice needs; problems of scale; problems of measurement and accountability.

COMPETENCY 3

Evaluate the extent to which the objectives and the intervention plan were achieved.

Fundamental Skills

1. Involving client populations in practice activities—skill in obtaining feedback from the client system about the degree to which the objectives of the intervention plan were achieved; involving the client system in the initial determination of evaluation criteria, methods, and time frame; making special efforts to involve the involuntary client as much as possible.

2. Involving others—skill in involving colleagues and relevant others in the initial determination of evaluation criteria, methods, and time frame; obtaining feedback from colleagues and relevant others as appropriate about the degree to which the objectives of the intervention plan were achieved.
3. Specifying behavior—skill in being able to specify the behaviors-events that will be used as indicators, whether or not the objectives of the intervention plan were achieved.
4. Specifying time limits for intervention—skill in being able to specify a time frame within which behaviors-events being used as indicators will be measured and evaluated.
5. Developing research variables—skill in being able to translate behaviors-events being used as indicators into measurable variables about which data can be collected.
6. Selecting a research strategy—skill in being able to select a research methodology appropriate to the behaviors-events to be measured for evaluation purposes.
7. Carrying out research activities—skill in carrying out basic research activities on one's own for evaluative purposes; collaborating with others in carrying out larger scale research activities that relate to the evaluation of the extent to which the objectives of the intervention plans within one's own workload were achieved.
8. Using consultation appropriately—skill in consulting with colleagues about the results of the intervention effort; discussing alternative or additional interventive strategies with colleagues; evaluating one's own activities in participating in interventive strategies with colleagues.
9. Renegotiating contracts—skill in involving the client system in planning new objectives and/or new activities as appropriate given the evaluation of the previous contract and its results; being as sensitive as possible to the needs and preferences of the involuntary client and involving him or her in the contracting process as much as possible.

Conceptual Knowledge

1. Research (see Competency 1, section 10, for this concept, and subsections 10 a-f).
   a. Problem formulation
   b. Information gathering
   c. Data collection
   d. Data analysis
   e. Organization of results

f. Evaluative research
2. Values (see Competency 1, section 2, for this concept, and subsections 2 a-c).
   a. Cultural values and their impact on social organization
   b. Group values and behavior patterns
   c. Professional ethics
3. Social change (see Competency 1, section 9, for this concept, and subsection 9a: see Competency 2, section 5, subsections 5 g-i, for b-d listed here).
   a. Problem-solving process
   b. Citizen participation in program implementation
   c. Self-help as a helping approach
   d. Contracting
4. Interpersonal influence (see Competency 2, section 4, for this concept and subsections 4 c-e, for a-c listed here).
   a. Situationally specific social work intervention strategies
   b. Intervention roles and activities
   c. Practice literature
5. Formal organization (see Competency 2, section 6, for this concept, and subsection 6g for a listed here).
   a. Principles of teamwork
   b. Consultation—knowledge of persons-groups from whom to appropriately seek consultation as specified by the organizational structure; persons-groups whose professional expertise make them appropriate persons-groups from whom to seek consultation informally; information and questions to be collected-prepared in advance of the consultation; use of self to avoid nonproductive resistence to seeking or making use of the results of consultation; the distinction between seeking consultation and having someone else solve one's problems.

COMPETENCY 4

Contribute to the improvement of service delivery by adding to the knowledge base of the profession as appropriate and by supporting and upholding the standards and ethics of the profession.

Fundamental Skills

1. Joining professional associations—skill in seeking information about relevant professional associations; accepting responsibility for professional activities by joining professional associations and participating in their activities.

2. Collecting data—skill in collecting data relevant to activities of professional social workers and the professional association; using appropriate research-data collection methods.
3. Analyzing data—skill in analyzing data to demonstrate professional activities and their effects; analyzing data to identify weaknesses or gaps in professional functioning.
4. Clarifying professional standards—skill in analyzing professional documents to understand them; interpreting professional standards to others; participating in activities to reject instances of unethical behavior; continuously using professional standards in the assessment of one's own practice and other professional activities.
5. Collaborating with professional colleagues—skill in identifying and participating in accessible and relevant organized groups of colleagues; sharing information with colleagues; accepting responsibility for carrying out mutually agreed upon group tasks; supporting the work of one's colleagues.
6. Organizing professional activities—skill in organizing activities desired by professional associations (such as membership meetings, workshops); organizing appearances before relevant persons and groups to provide information about or advocate for professional standards.
7. Presenting data—skill in using data to prepare reports, briefs, budgets, and documents as needed; transmitting data in appropriate form to professional association membership (in whole or part); transmitting data in appropriate form to persons outside the profession; presenting data in verbal form through lectures, committee appearances, media appearances, and so forth.
8. Continuing professional growth—skill in seeking information about relevant continuing education programs and opportunities; participating in continuing education as appropriate; using continuing education content to modify and enrich one's own practice and other professional activities.
9. Writing effectively for professional communication—skill in preparing available data obtained during one's own practice experience for presentation in professional journals or books as appropriate; writing clearly and succinctly.

Conceptual Knowledge

1. Research (see Competency 1, section 10, for this concept, and subsections 10a-f).
   a. Problem formulation
   b. Information gathering
   c. Data collection

    d. Data analysis

    e. Organization of results

    f. Evaluative research

    g. Ethics of research

2. Communication (see Competency 1, section 7, for this concept, and subsections 7a-f).

    a. Form of communication and clarity of transmission

    b. Communication within and between groups

    c. Purposes of communication

    d. Interviewing

    e. Nonverbal communication

    f. Recording

3. Values (see Competency 1, section 2, for this concept, and subsection 2c for a listed here).

    a. Professional ethics

4. Social change (see Competency 1, section 9, for this concept, and subsections 9a and b; see Competency 2, section 5, subsections 5c, d, and f, listed here as c-e).

    a. Problem-solving process

    b. Policy analysis

    c. Social planning process

    d. Policy formation

    e. Networks of professional organizations.

    f. Legislative processes—knowledge of governmental decision-making processes at the federal, state, and local levels; methods of providing input into legislative processes; points at which input is possible; distinction between the passage of legislation and the development of regulations to implement it.

    g. Organizing special interest groups—knowledge of the uses of special interest groups; methods of identifying existing or potential special interest groups; techniques for facilitating communication and/or structural development in special interest groups; methods for introducing information into these groups; strategies for providing support, technical assistance, and leadership to special interest groups; methods for clarifying relationships and mutual interests of special interest groups; techniques for promoting collaborative actions between special interest groups.

    h. Preparation of material for public dissemination—knowledge of basic report-writing skills; formats to use in preparing material for specific purposes and audiences; sources of data-knowledge about professional activities and/or service needs to use in preparation of material.

5. Formal organizations (see Competency 2, section 6, for this con-

cept, and subsections 6b, c, e, g, for a-d listed here; see Competency 3, section 5, subsection 5b, (listed here as e).
   a. Principles of organizational functioning
   b. Organizations as systems
   c. Interaction and communication patterns in organizations
   d. Principles of teamwork
   e. Consultation
   f. Professional association information—knowledge of professional association(s)' ethics; by-laws; membership procedures; resources; activities and benefits; meeting times and place.
   g. Professional roles—knowledge of appropriate activities when representing professional organization(s); strategies for integrating practice skills with activities on behalf of professional organization(s).
   h. Planning and carrying out membership activities—knowledge of procedures to obtain feedback from membership about their program preferences; strategies for relating program content to professional issues; resources to use on programs or in other activities.
   i. Employee utilization—knowledge of professional employee standards and utilization; procedures for securing employment in public and private agencies; use of professional employment standards by one's own agency and by other agencies in the community; grievance procedures established by professional organizations to protect professional standards.
6. Interpersonal influence (see Competency 1, section 8, for this concept, and subsection 8a; see Competency 2, section 4, subsections 4b and f, for b and c listed here).
   a. Relationship
   b. Group communication and decisionmaking
   c. Reinforcement
   d. Principles of leadership—knowledge of sources of influence; types of leadership; relationship of leadership type to group goals.
7. Teaching/Learning—knowledge of the process of learning (modeling, reinforcement, extinction); cognitive, affective, and skill learning; the impact of the learning environment; teaching techniques; appropriate teaching techniques for specified types of content to be taught and learning conditions (environment).
   a. The use of existing knowledge—knowledge of strategies for helping people use relevant knowledge that they already have; different knowledge bases likely to exist in different cultural and lifestyle groups; strategies for helping people distinguish be-

tween the knowledge they have and effective factors affecting
its use.

b. Planning and carrying out educational activities—knowledge of
procedures to obtain feedback from membership about their
educational needs and priorities; methods for selecting and organizing educational content; procedures for structuring learning experiences and resources; special educational needs of adult
learners; techniques for preparing educational materials.

c. Principles of effective teaching—knowledge of developing teaching-learning objectives; sources of information about the teaching-learning process; sources of information about specific
knowledge areas; varieties of teaching methodologies and appropriate circumstances for their use; developing appropriate evaluation instruments.

d. Teaching effectively—knowledge of strategies for relating teaching-learning objectives to characteristics of specific populations;
strategies for getting learner feedback in specified types of
teaching-learning situations.

COMPETENCY 5

Enhance the problem-solving, coping, and developmental capacities
of people.

Fundamental Skills

1. Understanding human diversity—skill in recognizing cultural and
   lifestyle traditions held by individuals and groups; recognizing
   the salience of cultural traditions for individuals and groups.

2. Using human diversity as a practice resource—skill in analyzing
   helping networks in diverse groups; analyzing perceptions about
   outside helping networks and persons held by members of diverse groups; developing effective strategies to interrelate natural helping networks with formally structured societal helping
   resources.

3. Respecting others—skill in managing one's own beliefs and
   values in order to be able to respect others whose cultural and
   lifestyle traditions and behaviors are different from one's own;
   managing one's own beliefs and values so that they do not interfere with effective planning and intervention with and on behalf
   of others.

4. Utilizing one's own professional self—skill in recognizing and
   analyzing one's own beliefs and values; using oneself in ways

compatible with professional ethics; using oneself in planned, helpful ways when functioning as a professional social worker.

5. Supporting others—skill in recognizing instances in which support is needed due to stresses caused by life cycle strains, resource needs, institutional malfunction, or interpersonal crises; providing support in helpful ways that utilize individual or group strengths; avoiding the generation of dependency relationships.

6. Teaching others—skill in recognizing the need for new information or skills; building on the information and skills that individuals and groups already have; teaching in ways compatible with the situation and with the cultural-lifestyle backgrounds of individuals and groups; distinguishing between teaching, counselling, and therapy.

7. Motivating others—skill in reinforcing the perceptions of individuals and groups that they have useful knowledge and skills; helping individuals and groups make use of the knowledge and skill available; using existing knowledge and skill as a base for seeking other needed resources and/or for developing additional knowledge and skills.

8. Involving others—skill in teaching others the value of their participation in planning and carrying out plans to the fullest extent possible; exploring the extent to which involuntary clients can be involved; providing a context of interaction that facilitates and rewards the involvement of others.

9. Developing awareness of others—skill in being sensitive to people's aspirations and goals; defining helping objectives as developmental and enriching as well as problem-solving; recognizing life cycle forces affecting needs, resources, and objectives at different points in individual, group, and community development.

10. Developing facility in problem solving—skill in identifying problems; partializing problems for planning and intervention purposes; prioritizing problems and their subparts; recognizing crisis situations and intervening appropriately; involving others as appropriate throughout the problem-solving process.

11. Developing understanding—skill in helping others understand the conditions that they find difficult or troublesome; helping others to see relationships between behaviors and conditions.

12. Facilitating interaction—skill in linking people with similar interests, needs, or concerns; promoting interaction among people with similar interests, needs, and concerns; providing assistance as requested and appropriate in the formulation, development, and use of group organization among people

with similar interests, needs, and concerns; promoting helpful interaction between groups, and clarifying issues and reducing conflicts where appropriate and desired.

13. Interacting with others—skill in relating comfortably to others individually and in groups; modeling and otherwise facilitating helpful interaction patterns between people.

14. Helping others develop positive self-images—skill in helping others recognize their own aspirations, traditions, and self-identity; helping others accept themselves and the things about themselves they like and dislike; helping others to find supports for their positive sense of self and resources to help them change aspects of self they may wish to change.

Conceptual Knowledge

1. Personal and group identity—knowledge of the concept of personal and group identity; identity as a component of personality development and functioning; processes of identity formation; processes of identity destruction.

   a. Human development—knowledge of the interplay between biological, psychological, and social forces in human development; the life cycle, with the tasks and risks built into each phase; resources needed at each stage in the life cycle; professional roles appropriate at each stage in the life cycle; major theories of human development; changing life circumstances and their effects on behaviors.

   b. Personality development and functioning—knowledge of major theories of personality development; problematic patterns of personality functioning; professional roles appropriate in problematic situations created by dysfunctional personality behavior patterns.

   c. Group development and functioning—knowledge of the importance of groups for individual socialization and functioning; types of groups; use of group structure and process to affect individual functioning; effects of problems in group functioning.

   d. Self-concept—knowledge of processes affecting the development of a stable self-concept; the importance of behavior modeling; processes affecting positive self-concept development and maintenance; use of interpersonal and group resources to strengthen self-concept; relationship between material resources, rewarding social experiences, and self-concept; effects of weak or negative self-concept.

      e. The human diversity continuum—knowledge of the range that exists no matter what the area of behavior; strategies for recognizing where an individual or group falls along a behavioral continuum; understanding behavioral continuums within as well as between groups; understanding behavioral continuums with respect to racial, ethnic, cultural, sexual, sexual preference, lifestyle, and physical ability groups.

      f. Cultural and lifestyle traditions—knowledge of the importance of knowledge of and respect for cultural and lifestyle traditions for identity and self-concept formation; effects of loss or rejection of cultural and lifestyle traditions.

2. Culture (see Competency 1, section 1, for this concept, and subsections 1a and b).
   a. Cultural relativity
   b. Cultural transition

3. Values (see Competency 1, section 2, for this concept, and subsections 2a-d).
   a. Cultural values and their impact on social organization
   b. Group values and behavior patterns
   c. Professional ethics
   d. Personal values and ethics

4. Social problems (see Competency 1, section 3, for this concept, and subsections 3a-c).
   a. Describing social problems
   b. Major social problems
   c. Effects of social problems

5. Social institutions (see Competency 1, section 4, for this concept, and subsections 4a-c).
   a. Major social institutions
   b. The social welfare institution
   c. Social work as a profession

6. Social system (see Competency 1, section 5, for this concept, and subsection 5a).
   a. The structure of resource and delivery systems

7. Community (see Competency 1, section 6, for this concept, and subsections 6a and b).
   a. Group responses to need
   b. Community change

8. Communication (see Competency 1, section 7, for this concept, and subsections 7a-e).
   a. Form of communication and clarity of transmission
   b. Communication within and between groups

    c. Purposes of communication

    d. Interviewing

    e. Nonverbal communication

9. Interpersonal influence (see Competency 1, section 8, for this concept, and subsection 8a; see Competency 2, section 4, for subsections 4b-f).

    a. Relationship

    b. Group communication and decisionmaking

    c. Situationally specific social work interventive strategies

    d. Interventive roles and activities

    e. Practice literature

    f. Reinforcement.

10. Social change (see Competency 1, section 9, for this concept, and subsection 9a; see Competency 2, for subsections 5c, g, h, and i, here listed as b-e).

    a. Problem-solving process

    b. Social planning process

    c. Citizen participation in program implementation

    d. Self-help as a helping approach

    e. Contracting

11. Social differentation—knowledge of the concepts of social differentiation and social stratification; major critera used to differentiate (race, ethnicity, sex, age, socioeconomic status, sexual preference); the functions and dysfunctions of differentiation.

    a. Social differentiation and the creation of majority-minority groups—knowledge of the effect of social differentiation on labeling; labeling and the creation of prejudice and discrimination; minority status and life chances and lifestyle; labeling and its effects on the creation and provision of social welfare services-resources.

    b. Social differentiation and self-concept formation—knowledge of minority status and denigration of self; group cohesion and reinforcement of self-image; group cohesion and countervailing power; self-concept and need for social welfare services-resources.

    c. Social stratification and social class—knowledge of the use of socioeconomic resources to create social classes; behavioral correlates of social class; correlation of social class, race, ethnicity, sex, and physical handicaps; social class and economic exploitation; social class and alienation.

12. Teaching/Learning (see Competency 4, section 7, for this concept, and subsections 7a, c, and d, listed here as a-c).

a. The use of existing knowledge
b. Principles of effective teaching
c. Teaching effectively

COMPETENCY 6

Link people with systems that provide them with resources, services, and opportunities.

Fundamental Skills

1. Obtaining information—skill at contacting persons or checking materials to clarify eligibility criteria and/or application procedures.
2. Determining eligibility—skill at being able to assess the suitability of a person-group for services-resources that have specified eligibility conditions.
3. Providing information—skill at making information available to persons-groups about available services-resources and to service-resource providers about potential users.
4. Referring persons—skill at helping persons identify and reach services-resources located outside of one's own agency.
5. Providing support—skill at helping persons-groups understand and adjust to one's own agency and helping them apply for services-resources with technical as well as affective support.
6. Facilitating organizational functioning—skill at helping persons-groups use the organizational structure of one's own agency effectively to obtain appropriate resources, services, opportunities.
7. Translating communications—skill at helping persons understand the meaning of verbal and written communications and also to express their intentions more clearly.
8. Mediating—skill at facilitating interaction between individuals and groups and especially between individuals-groups and providers of services-resources.
9. Monitoring service delivery—skill at examining individual-group and service delivery system interaction to identify inappropriate, discriminatory, or unhelpful service-interaction events.
10. Motivating—skill at stimulating people to find their own resources and to make better use of available services-resources, as well as reducing unnecessary dependency on the helping person.

Conceptual Knowledge

1. Culture (see Competency 1, section 1, for this concept, and sub-sections 1a and b).
    a. Cultural relativity
    b. Cultural transition
2. Values (see Competency 1, section 2, for this concept, and sub-sections 2a-d).
    a. Cultural values and their impact on social organization
    b. Group values and behavior patterns
    c. Professional ethics
    d. Personal values and ethics
3. Roles—knowledge of the concepts of role, position, and status; the multiplicity of roles and the potential for role conflicts; role performance and individual variation in role behavior; the functions and dysfunctions of roles; the allocation of positions and roles.
    a. Positions and roles in groups, especially formal organizations—knowledge of issues involved when positions and roles are increased, decreased, or changed; potential conflicts arising between positions and roles; strategies for reducing position-role conflicts.
    b. Role performance of organizational members—knowledge of values and role performance; role performance and achievement or distortion of organizational goals; individual interpretation of organizational procedures and impact on service delivery.
4. Social differentiation (see Competency 5, section 11, for this concept, and subsections 11a-c).
    a. Social differentiation and the creation of minority-majority groups
    b. Social differentiation and self-concept formation
    c. Social stratification and social class
5. Social power—knowledge of the concepts of power and influence; the major bases of socially allocated and individual power; social institutions and the management of power.
    a. Power and social differentiation—interaction between social differentiation and access to power; common uses of power for exploitative purposes (with particular attention to minority groups).
6. Social system (see Competency 1, section 5, for this concept, and subsections 5a and c).

    a. The structure of resource and delivery systems

    b. Resource information—knowledge about helpful sources of information when seeking to identify resources, services, and opportunities.

    c. Comparative social welfare systems

7. Community (see Competency 1, section 6, for this concept, and subsections 6a and b).

    a. Group responses to need

    b. Community change

8. Formal organizations (see Competency 2, section 6, for this concept, and subsection 6a).

    a. Organizational procedures affecting formal and informal access mechanisms

9. Communication (see Competency 1, section 7, for this concept, and subsections 7a and b).

    a. Form of communication and clarity of transmission

    b. Communication within and between groups

10. Personal and group identity (see Competency 5, section 1 for this concept).

    a. Self-help as a helping approach—knowledge of values supporting self-help; relationship of self-help to structured helping programs; self-help and the need for resources.

11. Teaching/learning (see Competency 4, section 7, for this concept, and subsection 7a).

    a. The use of existing knowledge

    b. Teaching about resources, services, and opportunities—knowledge of strategies for most effectively providing information about relevant resources, services, and opportunities, using written and electronic media as appropriate; uses of groups for teaching-learning purposes, especially as relates to affective and skill knowledge concerning resources, services, and service delivery structures; strategies to develop and use an awareness of indigenous helping networks; different teaching-learning strategies appropriate to diverse groups.

COMPETENCY 7

Promote the effective and humane operation of the systems that provide people with services, resources, and opportunities.

Fundamental Skills

1. Obtaining feedback—skill at assessing the impact of helping systems on people by obtaining information from those affected by such systems.

2. Obtaining information—skill at using available sources of information to assess the impact of helping systems on people.
3. Analyzing organizational policy—skill in applying policy analysis frameworks to organizational policies and policymaking structures; relating policy to professional roles in the organization; relating policy to the provision of services by the agency.
4. Using organizational procedures—skill in using formal and informal organizational procedures appropriately and effectively to achieve service objectives or changes in service delivery procedures-objectives.
5. Using communication channels—skill in the use of formal and informal communication channels to facilitate service delivery and/or organizational change.
6. Using organizational ambiguity—skill in identifying and using ambiguities and/or gaps in the organizational structure to facilitate service delivery and/or organizational change.
7. Relating to colleagues—skill in being sensitive to the needs of colleagues, including supervisors and administrators, providing support where appropriate.
8. Developing a collegial network—skill in identifying and organizing a network of colleagues in an organization that can be used to collectively achieve and/or uphold professional standards.
9. Helping colleagues—skill in facilitating the work of professional colleagues.
10. Using personal power—skill in demonstrating one's professional effectiveness within the organization; using one's professional competence to bargain within the organization for resources needed to improve one's own or the organization's service delivery; participating in decisionmaking when in a position to do so; expressing opinions and recommendations to those in decisionmaking positions.
11. Using systems—skill in identifying individuals, groups, systems, outside the organization that can be useful in helping an organization achieve its service objectives; facilitating positive communication and relationships between organizations and useful outside individuals, groups, systems; mobilizing the resources of outside individuals, groups, systems.
12. Using conflict and confrontation—skill in identifying situations in which regular procedures for influence within an organization are ineffective; assessing the costs of using conflict and/or confrontation; assessing the relative strengths of the groups involved in a conflict and/or confrontation effort; mobilizing the power of groups to affect organizational functioning.
13. Maintaining professional identity—skill in maintaining clarity

for oneself about professional ethics and professional self-identity, regardless of agency setting or organizational pressures.

14. Interpreting professional roles—skill in clarifying appropriate professional activities and ethics to others in an organization; rejecting and/or negotiating inappropriate expectations by an organization.

Conceptual Knowledge

1. Values (see Competency 1, section 2, for this concept, and subsections 2a and b).
   a. Cultural values and their impact on social organization.
   b. Group values and behavior patterns
   c. Professional ethics—knowledge of professional ethics; use of accountability to user groups as part of professional self-evaluation and evaluation of services-resources.
2. Research (see Competency 1, section 10, for this concept, and subsections 10a-g).
   a. Problem formulation
   b. Information gathering
   c. Data collection
   d. Data analysis
   e. Organization of results
   f. Evaluative research
   g. Ethics of research with human subjects
3. Formal organizations (see Competency 2, section 6, for this concept, and subsections 6a-h, listed here as a-f; and k).
   a. Organizational procedures affecting formal and informal mechanisms
   b. Principles of organizational functioning
   c. Organizations as systems
   d. Organizational goals
   e. Interaction and communication patterns in organizations
   f. Power relations in organizations
   g. Sources of negotiation in organizations—knowledge of professional competence as a bargaining tool; use of internal collegial networks; use of external power bases; use of access to needed resources.
   h. Organizational change—knowledge of formal and informal change structures; internally and externally motivated change; gaps or ambiguities in structure and their change potential.
   i. Frameworks for organizational policy analysis—knowledge of policymaking as an organizational function; structured policy-

making procedures; informal input into policymaking; impact of external systems.
  j. Principles of teamwork
  k. Practice objectives and service structures

COMPETENCY 8

Make special efforts on behalf of populations most vulnerable and discriminated against.

Fundamental Skills

1. Utilizing one's own professional self—skill at understanding one's own feelings and attitudes about human diversity; understanding one's own feelings and attitudes about specific groups and their members.
2. Respecting others—skill at understanding and respecting the needs and preferences of others; individualizing others regardless of cultural or lifestyle group membership and attendant stereotypes; respecting alternative modes of expression and use of resources by members of diverse groups.
3. Hearing—skill at understanding and/or interpreting the meaning of client system comments about service delivery systems; facilitating the expression of comments, feelings, and opinions by all parts of the client system.
4. Using professional ethics—skill at using professional social work ethics as a framework for assessing social conditions and human services; using professional ethics to define appropriate activities for oneself in identifying problematic social conditions of the service delivery system; using knowledge of professional ethics to identify instances of violations of them by individuals or organizations.
5. Collecting data—skill at using appropriate data collection methods to extract data from one's own caseload pertinent to the demonstration of unmet or inadequately met needs.
6. Analyzing and organizing data—skill at analyzing data collected from one's own caseload; organizing caseload data in the most effective way to demonstrate unmet or inadequately met needs.
7. Reaching out to client populations—skill at using data to identify diverse groups; initiating contact with members of such groups; identifying unmet needs or systematic disadvantage in such groups.
8. Using indigenous helping networks—skill at recognizing in-

digenous helping networks; utilizing other services-resources to supplement and support indigenous helping networks; helping group members learn about, make contact with, and use indigenous helping networks; helping members of diverse groups develop indigenous helping networks when feasible and desirable.

9. Developing collegial support networks—skill in identifying colleagues interested in reducing service inequalities and inhumane procedures; sharing data demonstrating these conditions with them; facilitating their own data collection about these conditions; facilitating communication and planning among these colleagues.

10. Developing community support networks—skill in identifying community persons and/or decisionmakers interested in reducing service inequalities and inhumane procedures; sharing data demonstrating these conditions with them; facilitating their own data collection about these conditions from agencies, printed sources, and consumers; facilitating communication and planning among these persons.

11. Advocating—skill at utilizing agency procedures, policymaking contexts, the media, and collegial and community support networks to achieve change in policies and structures affecting services-resources and the way they are delivered to persons-groups from populations most vulnerable and discriminated against.

12. Communicating effectively—skill in transmitting information about service inequalities and inhumane procedures verbally, in written form, and through the media.

13. Assessing one's own intervention activities—skill at using collected data to assess one's own practice to identify instances of services inequalities and inhumane procedures.

Conceptual Knowledge

1. Culture (see Competency 1, section 1, for this concept and subsection 1a).
    a. Cultural relativity

2. Values (see Competency 1, section 2, for this concept, and subsections 2a and b).
    a. Cultural values and their impact on social organization
    b. Group values and behavior patterns
    c. Professional social work ethics—knowledge of ethical standards for structuring services, dealing with people, and acting responsibly as a social work professional.
    d. Social welfare values—knowledge of major social welfare

values; relationships with other significant societal values; relationships with values of major cultural and lifestyle groups.

   e. Societal values and social welfare programs—knowledge of the impact societal values have on which programs are proposed and implemented; societal values and the way in which programs are offered; societal values and services to major cultural and lifestyle groups.

3. Social differentiation (see Competency 5, section 11, for this concept, and subsections 11a and b).
    a. Social differentiation and the creation of majority-minority groups
    b. Social differentiation and self-concept formation
    c. Effects of social differentiation—knowledge of the effects of group membership on life chances and lifestyles.

4. Social power (see Competency 6, section 5, for this concept, and subsection 5a).
    a. Power and social differentiation
    b. Effects of power and influence structures—knowledge of the effects of group membership on need; access to power and ability to meet needs; access to power and participation in social welfare planning.

5. Social system (see Competency 1, section 5, for this concept, and subsection 1a).
    a. The structure of resource and service delivery systems
    b. Service gaps and biases—knowledge of the gaps in services existing in the structure of social welfare programs; service delivery problems; special problems faced by members of diverse groups.

6. Community (see Competency 1, section 6, for this concept, and subsection 6a).
    a. Group responses to need

7. Formal organization (see Competency 2, section 6, for this concept, and subsection 6a).
    a. Organizational procedures affecting formal and informal access mechanisms

8. Communication (see Competency 1, section 7, for this concept, and subsections 7a and b).
    a. Form of communication and clarity of transmission
    b. Communication within and between groups
    c. Techniques of persuasive communication—knowledge of effective techniques to reach audiences; methods of presenting different types of messages; basic verbal skills; basic writing skills.
    d. Knowledge dissemination channels—knowledge of major

channels through which data about unmet need and/or service gaps and inequality can be disseminated; form in which data must be packaged for each communication channel.

  e. Influence networks—knowledge of persons, groups, organizations, to whom data should be directed; form in which data must be packaged to be useable by each person, group, organization.

 9. Personal and group identity (see Competency 5, section 1, for this concept, and Competency 6, subsection 6a).

  a. Self-help as a helping approach

  b. Basic human needs—knowledge of the needs that people have in order to grow and function with integrity and personal satisfaction; the effects when certain needs are not met; variations in need expression and priorities of needs among major cultural and lifestyle groups.

  c. Group membership and identity—knowledge of group identity as a human need; social differentiation and the denigration of groups; group denigration and impact on group disorganization; group denigration and impact on provision of services (type and method of provision) for group members.

 10. Social Problems (see Competency 1, section 3, for this concept, and subsections 3a-d).

  a. Describing social problems

  b. Major social problems

  c. Effects of social problems

  d. Social problems and social welfare services-resources

 11. Research (see Competency 1, section 10, for this concept, and subsections 10 b-e, here listed as a-d).

  a. Information gathering

  b. Data collection

  c. Data analysis

  d. Organization of results

COMPETENCY 9

Actively participate with others in creating new, modified or improved service, resource, opportunity, systems that are more equitable, just, and responsive to consumers of services.

Fundamental Skills

 1. Utilizing one's own professional self—skill in understanding one's own commitment to social justice; one's own commit-

ment to using oneself to achieve improved social resources and services; one's own attitudes toward members of different cultural and lifestyle groups; one's own attitude toward those in positions of power.

2. Clarifying attitudes and feelings—skill in assisting others to clarify their attitudes toward social justice; their feelings toward service users; their feelings toward members of diverse groups; their commitment to working for improved social resources and services.

3. Clarifying implications of choices—skill in helping others understand the implications of their attitudes and feelings on service delivery; helping others understand the implications of their working or not working for social justice.

4. Supporting professional ethics—skill in providing information about professional ethics during planning and implementation activities; clarifying the implications of professional ethics in specific situations; personally rejecting activities or plans contrary to professional ethics; encouraging others to reject unethical activities or plans.

5. Involving others—skill in identifying potential participants; making contact with potential participants; informing such persons of potential activities; supporting and assisting others in their activities; insuring the participation of involuntary client groups as far as possible.

6. Respecting others—skill in understanding the attitudes, feelings, and behaviors of others; separating disagreements about attitudes, feelings, and behaviors from denigration of the person; understanding the person's context for his or her attitudes, feelings, and behaviors.

7. Working collaboratively with others—skill in identifying common interests and activities; clarifying the division of labor possible and desirable; helping others perform their activities when possible and desired by them; communicating in ways understandable and acceptable to others.

8. Supporting activities by citizen groups—skill in providing information; the performance of activities; goal clarification; supporting and encouraging attitudes and behaviors compatible with goal attainment.

9. Developing collegial support networks—skill in identifying colleagues interested in improving services-resources; sharing data demonstrating the need for improvement-change; facilitating their own data collection about the need for improvement-change; facilitating communication and planning among these colleagues.

10. Developing community support networks—skill in identifying community persons and/or decisionmakers interested in the provision of more effective social welfare services-resources; sharing data demonstrating the need for improved services-resources with them; facilitating their own data collection about the need for more effective services from agencies; printed sources, and consumers; facilitating communication and planning among these persons.

11. Communicating effectively—skill in written communication; skill in verbal communication; communicating using styles-media appropriate to the message; identifying appropriate targets for one's communication; communicating using styles-media appropriate to one's audience(s).

12. Answering questions and providing information—skill in answering questions; providing information when needed or requested.

13. Planning and policy participation—skill in the analysis of relevant planning and policy contexts and structures; participation in planning and policy activities as appropriate; use of legislative and agency policy and planning arenas to work toward more effective services and service delivery.

14. Presenting plans—skill in presenting plans to appropriate audiences; providing clarification of parts of the plan as needed.

15. Identifying types of plans—skill in distinguishing between power-based and service-based planning; clarifying planning objectives; clarifying professional ethics as they apply to planning.

16. Summarizing content—skill in summarizing discussions; summarizing other data and information; extracting information from data and other sources.

17. Promoting communication—skill in facilitating communication within a group; facilitating communication between groups; clarifying objectives; clarifying points of confusion.

18. Providing feedback—skill in transmitting information about planning and change activities to interested and/or affected client systems.

Conceptual Knowledge

1. Social change (see Competency 1, section 9, for this concept, and subsection 9a; see Competency 2, section 5, subsections 5c-g, for b-f listed here).
   a. Problem-solving process
   b. Social planning process
   c. Policy formation

    d. Networks of social agencies
    e. Networks of professional organizations
    f. Citizen participation in program implementation
2. Interpersonal influence (see Competency 1, section 8, for this concept; see Competency 2, section 4, subsection 4b).
    a. Behavior change—knowledge of techniques of behavior change (modeling, reinforcement, extinction); environmental conditions affecting behavior change techniques; behavioral inhibition and disinhibition.
    b. Group communication and decisionmaking
3. Community (see Competency 1, section 6, for this concept, and subsection 6a).
    a. Group responses to need
    b. Community influence and power structures—knowledge of types of communities; common power bases in different types of communities; sources of access to community influentials; political processes at the community level and their relationships with state and national politics.
4. Social power (see Competency 6, section 5, for this concept, and subsection 5a; see Competency 8, section 4, subsection 4b).
    a. Power and social differentiation
    b. Effects of power and influence structures
    c. Power structures and the structure of social welfare services—knowledge of power structures with interest in social welfare resources; conflicts of interest between power structures and social welfare service structures; points for negotiation and compromise; strategies for cooptation, confrontation, competition, and cooperation.
5. Research (see Competency 1, section 10, for this concept, and subsections 10b-f listed here as a-e).
    a. Information gathering
    b. Data collection
    c. Data analysis
    d. Organization of results
    e. Evaluative research
6. Values (see Competency 1, section 2, for this concept and subsections 2a and b; see Competency 8, section 2, subsections 2c-e).
    a. Cultural values and their impact on social organization
    b. Group values and behavior patterns
    c. Professional social work ethics
    d. Social welfare values
    e. Societal values and social welfare programs

7. Social differentiation (see Competency 5, section 11, for this concept, and subsections 11a and b; see Competency 8, section 3, subsection 3c).
   a. Social differentiation and the creation of majority-minority groups.
   b. Social differentiation and self-concept formation
   c. Effects of social differentiation
8. Social system (see Competency 1, section 5, for this concept, and subsection 5a; see Competency 8, section 5, subsection 5b).
   a. The structure of resource and service delivery systems
   b. Service gaps and biases
9. Formal organization (see Competency 2, section 6, for this concept, and subsection 6a).
   a. Organizational procedures affecting formal and informal access mechanisms
10. Communication (see Competency 1, section 7, for this concept, and subsections 7a and b; see Competency 8, section 8, subsections 8c-e).
    a. Form of communication and clarity of transmission
    b. Communication within and between groups
    c. Techniques of persuasive communication
    d. Knowledge dissemination channels
    e. Influence networks

COMPETENCY 10

Continually evaluates one's own professional growth and development through assessment of practice behaviors and skills.

Fundamental Skills

1. Developing behavioral indicators—skill in identifying objectively measurable as well as more subjective indicators useable in collecting data about practice outcomes.
2. Collaborating with client populations—skill in engaging client populations in the evaluation process by seeking data from them and by mutually discussing the interpretation of the data to be used in the evaluation process.
3. Using appropriate research methodologies—skill in selecting and using appropriate data collection and analysis techniques for the type of data available and/or needed.
4. Collecting data—skill in periodically reviewing interventive activities-records to collect data as indicated by behavioral indicators and research methology(s) selected.

5. Interpreting and using data—skill in summarizing and analyzing data in order to reach conclusions about one's practice effectiveness; skill in integrating data about one's own practice into ongoing activity without dysfunctional emotional resistance; skill in using data about one's own practice to become more aware of one's own professional values and use of self.
6. Assessing situations—skill in assessing the impact of alternative intervention activities in specified situations.
7. Selecting alternatives—skill in selecting and/or developing alternative intervention strategies or plans consistent with assessment findings.
8. Renegotiating contracts—skill in renegotiating the interventive contract with the client system as appropriate, being sensitive to the affect that may be associated with contract renegotiation.
9. Using professional social work ethics—skill in translating social work ethics into a personal framework to evaluate one's own interventive effectiveness and professional development.
10. Managing professional resources—skill in managing time so as to be knowledgeable about current literature of importance to social work practice.

Conceptual Knowledge

1. Social change (see Competency 1, section 9, for this concept, and subsection 9a).
   a. Problem-solving process
   b. Strategies of professional intervention—knowledge of the helping skills used by social workers; a general knowledge of the helping skills used by other related professionals (to use for referrals when social work may not be the appropriate profession).
   c. Situationally specific social work intervention strategies—knowledge of interventive strategies possible and appropriate in specific practice situations.
   d. Interventive roles and activities—knowledge of the professional, client system, and resource system roles and activities appropriate for specific interventive strategies.
   e. Practice literature—knowledge of major sources of information; major findings in the practice literature about the effects of interventive strategies commonly used by baccalaureate level social workers.
2. Interpersonal influence (see Competency 1, section 8, for this concept, and subsection 9b; see Competency 2, section 4, subsections 4c-e, listed here as d-f; see Competency 9, section 2, subsection 2a).

a. Behavior change
b. Group communication and decisionmaking
c. Contracting—knowledge of the contracting process, including criteria and times for evaluation and assessment; strategies for involving client systems in the contract process.
d. Situationally specific social work intervention strategies
e. Intervention roles and activities
f. Practice literature
3. Values (see Competency 1, section 2, for this concept, and subsections 2a and b; see Competency 8, section 2, for subsections 2c-e).
a. Cultural values and their impact on social organization
b. Group values and behavior patterns
c. Professional social work ethics
d. Social welfare values
e. Societal values and social welfare programs
4. Research (see Competency 1, section 10, for this concept, and subsections 10b-f, listed here as a-e).
a. Information gathering
b. Data collection
c. Data analysis
d. Organization of results
e. Evaluative research

List of Resource Persons to the Project

Chauncey Alexander
National Association of Social Workers
Washington, D.C.

L. Diane Bernard
Florida State University
Tallahassee, Florida

Larry Betts
Sunny Ridge Home
Richmond, Virginia

Sung Lai Boo
West Virginia University
Morgantown, West Virginia

Ed Bouton
Department of Social Services
Montgomery County
Silver Spring, Maryland

Cynthia Brown
Clayton County Department of
    Family and Childrens Services
Jonesboro, Georgia

Ann Burds
State Department of Public Welfare
Helena, Montana

Kevin Burns
Iowa Department of Social Services
Des Moines, Iowa

Harry Butler
California State University
San Diego, California

James Chapman
Department of Public Welfare
Ogden, Utah

Angel Campos
State University of New York
Stoney Brook, New York

Millie M. Charles
Southern University
New Orleans, Louisiana

Betty Coates
Northeast Florida Area Agency on
    Aging
Jacksonville, Florida

Maurice Connery
University of California at Los Angeles
Los Angeles, California

Virgil Conrad
West Virginia Department of Welfare
Charleston, West Virginia

Robert Constable
University of Illinois, Chicago Circle
Chicago, Illinois

Kate Daley
Foster Parent
Chicago, Illinois

Randy De Frehn
United Mine Workers
New Kensington, Pennsylvania

Jeri Dell
Retired Senior Volunteer Program
Reno, Nevada

Debra De Witz
Human Services Center
Rugby, North Dakota

Richard Doran
Veterans Administration
Albany, New York

Loretta Dotson
Harris County Department of Social
  Services
Houston, Texas

James Dumpson
Council on Social Work Education
New York, New York

Charlotte Dunmore
University of Pittsburgh
Pittsburgh, Pennsylvania

Richard Edwards
National Association of Social Workers
Washington, D.C.

Steve Emerson
Ada County Juvenile Center
Boise, Idaho

Charles Farris
Barry College
Miami Shores, Florida

Philip Fellin
University of Michigan
Ann Abor, Michigan

Jo Fisher-Hall
Housing and Urban Development
U.S. Department of Health, Education
  and Welfare
Washington, D.C.

Susan Ford
Rape Crisis Center
Grand Forks, North Dakota

Murray Frank
American Federation of State, County,
  and Municipal Employees
New York, New York

Karen Freeman
Pueblo County Social Services
Pueblo, Colorado

Jeanine Fried
County Department of Social Services
Albuquerque, New Mexico

Larry Garcia
Social Service Agency
Las Vegas, New Mexico

James Gigante
Office of Manpower Development
Social and Rehabilitation Service
  Training
U.S. Department of Health, Education,
  and Welfare
Washington, D.C.

Leon Ginsberg*
West Virginia Department of Welfare
Charleston, West Virginia

Barbara Glaser
Department of Human Resources
Arlington, Virginia

Gale Goldberg
University of Louisville
Louisville, Kentucky

Charlotte Goodluck
Jewish Family Service
Phoenix, Arizona

Cynthianna Hahn
Chicago, Illinois

Maurice Hamovitch
University of Southern California
Los Angeles, California

  *Formerly at West Virginia
University.

Anita Harbert
West Virginia University
Morgantown, West Virginia

Alice Hinton
Department of Public Welfare
Philadelphia, Pennsylvania

Nancy Humphreys
Rutgers University
New Brunswick, New Jersey

Jeanne M. Hunzeker
West Virginia University
Morgantown, West Virginia

Lynn Jacobson
Division of Family Services
Provo, Utah

Herbert Jarrett
University of Georgia
Athens, Georgia

Robert Jones
West Virginia University
Morgantown, West Virginia

Howard Jones
Dede Wallace Mental Health Center
Nashville, Tennessee

Arthur Katz
University of Kansas
Manhattan, Kansas

Marilyn Kellner
Columbus Tenants' Union
Columbus, Ohio

Pearl Kleinberg*
University of Wyoming
Laramie, Wyoming

Stephanie Klopfleisch
Department of Public Social Services
El Monte, California

Diane Kravetz
University of Wisconsin
Madison, Wisconsin

*Formerly at West Virginia
University.

Paul Kusuda
Division of Corrections
Madison, Wisconsin

Jean Leonatti
Central Missouri Area Agency on
   Aging
Columbia, Missouri

Gary Lloyd
University of Houston
Houston, Texas

Richard Lodge
Council on Social Work Education
New York, New York

Frank M. Loewenberg
Bar-Ilan University
Ramat-Gan, Israel

Jeweldean Londa
National Urban League
New York, New York

Maryann Mahaffey
Wayne State University
Detroit, Michigan

Jess McDonald
Department of Children and Family
   Services
Springfield, Illinois

Demetria McJulien
Southern University
Baton Rouge, Louisiana

John J. McManus
AFL-CIO Department of Community
   Services
Washington, D.C.

William McQueen
United Way of America
Alexandria, Virginia

George Metrey
Kean College
Union, New Jersey

Carol H. Meyer
Columbia University
New York, New York

Ruth Middleman
University of Louisville
Lousiville, Kentucky

Anne Minahan
University of Wisconsin
Madison, Wisconsin .

Emelicia Mizio
Family Service Association of America
New York, New York

Miguel Monteil
Arizona State University
Tempe, Arizona

Kenji Murase
San Francisco State University
San Francisco, California

Barbara Murphy
Society for Hospital Social Workers
Bethesda, Maryland

Regina Nees
Foster Parent
Boston, Massachusetts

George Nishinaka
Special Services for Groups, Inc.
Los Angeles, California

Elizabeth Norris
Avila College
Kansas City, Missouri

Bartley Nourse
Boy Scouts of America
New Brunswick, New Jersey

Christine Nyberg
South Health Association
Tacoma, Washington

Raymond Olsen
American Correctional Association
College Park, Maryland

Allen Pincus
University of Wisconsin
Madison, Wisconsin

Paul Raymer
California State University
San Diego, California

Sylvia Quezada
Childrens Medical Center
Dallas, Texas

William Quick
Office of Family and Children and
   Adult Services
Olympia, Washington

May Roberts
Foster Parent
Des Moines, Iowa

Robert Roberts
University of Southern California
Los Angeles, California

Phyllis Rochelle
San Francisco State University
San Francisco, California

Jay Roney
Social Security Administration
Baltimore, Maryland

Elaine Rothenberg
Virginia Commonwealth University
Richmond, Virginia

Myrtle Reul
University of Georgia
Athens, Georgia

James Ryan
Milwaukee Regional Office–Public
   Welfare
Milwaukee, Wisconsin

Carl Scott
Council on Social Work Education
New York, New York

Barbara K. Shore
University of Pittsburgh
Pittsburgh, Pennsylvania

Carol Smith
Jefferson County Department of
   Pensions and Security
Birmingham, Alabama

John Spores
University of Montana
Missoula, Montana

Alfred Stamm
Council on Social Work Education
New York, New York

Len Stern
National Association of Social Workers
Washington, D.C.

Elinor Stevens
Council on Social Work Education
New York, New York

Nancy Stevens
Woodruff Community Hospital
Long Beach, California

Laurie Stewart
Rutland Opportunity Council
Rutland, Vermont

Robert Stewart
Timberlawn Hospital
Dallas, Texas

Jack Stumpf
California State University
San Diego, California

Clara Swan
Child Welfare League of America
New York, New York

Robert Teare
University of Alabama
Tuscaloosa, Alabama

M. Truehart Titzl
Spalding College
Louisville, Kentucky

Ray Valle
California State University
San Diego, California

Ione Vargas
Temple University
Philadelphia, Pennsylvania

Constance Williams
Metropolitan College-Boston
   University
Boston, Massachusetts

Dorothy Williams
National Foster Parents Association
St. Louis, Missouri

Theatrice Williams
Department of Corrections
Minneapolis, Minnesota

Milton Wittman
Alcohol, Drug Abuse, and Mental
   Health Administration
National Institute of Mental Health
Bethesda, Maryland

Jimmie Woodward
Young Women's Christian Association
   of the U.S.A.
New York, New York

Deborah Zinn
West Virginia Department of Welfare
Charleston, West Virginia

❉ Index

AA degree, 14
Accountability/responsibility, 44, 46, 55
  bureaucracy and, 53, 153, 156, 158, 163
  for change, 163
  of education, 177, 179, 181, 182
  faculty, 126, 180
  government agency, 181
  social worker, 61, 62, 121–122, 172–173, 176, 177, 182
  and "what's worth knowing," 137
Accreditation:
  CSWE Commission on, 19–21, 30, 44, 99
  CSWE standards of, 24, 30, 42, 61, 62–63, 143, 144, 146, 176
  and curriculum, 22–27 (passim), 100, 133 (see also Curriculum and curriculum content)
  and degree requirements, 141
ACSW (Certified Social Worker):
  certification, economic advantages of, 8
  classification established, 13
Activity(ies):
  defined, 64
  professional practice entry level (illustrative), 68, 70–84 (see also Practice; Profession, professionalism)
Administration:
  BSWs and, 56, 59
  and bureaucracy, see Bureaucracy
  of education, policy and procedure, 134, 142–145, 146
  nondirect service jobs in, 180
  and "physical place," 137, 138, 139 (see also Environment)
  -student relationships, 142–144
  work-management skills and, 178
AFDC children, 174, 177
Age and the aging, curriculum content and, 102
Albert Einstein Medical Center (Philadelphia), 11
Allport, Gordon W., 137
America. See United States

American Association for Organizing Family Social Work, 119
American Association of Social Workers (AASW), 119
American Medical Association, 118
American Public Welfare Association, 33, 40, 44, 51
Annals of the American Society of Political and Social Sciences, The, 118–119
"Assumptions" in study project, 43
  related to practice and the profession, 61–62
  related to social work education, 62–63

Baccalaureate social worker. *See* BSW(s)
Barker, Robert L., 11, 12
Bartlett, Harriet M., 115
Behavior:
  and behavioral expectations, response, 117, 120, 123 (see also Ethics, professional)
  and bureaucratic discretionary power, see Bureaucracy
  coping or adaptive, 79, 87, 127
  environment and, 140 (see also Environment)
  flexibility of, 179 (see also Change)
  and human diversity, see Diversity, human
  need for study of, in curriculum, 58
  role models and, 134–135, 145–146
  sociocultural effects on, 101 (see also Culture)
  See also Relationships
Bisno, Herbert, 35
Boehm, Werner W., 35, 69n.3
Briggs, Thomas L., 11, 12, 37
Brown, Malcolm J., 117
BSW(s):
  as administrators, 56, 59
  Association of, and curriculum-study workshop, 42, 51–52
  and bureaucracy, 152 (see also Bureaucracy)
  classification established, 13, 14